For
Hadil Hashlamoun

Publisher:

Dar al Janub
Union for Antiracism and Peace Policy

RECLAIMING PALESTINE

EMPOWERING THE MARGINALIZED –
THE SOCIAL AND ECONOMICAL RECONSTRUCTION OF
PALESTINIAN SOCIETY UNDER FOREIGN OCCUPATION

Bibliografische Information der Deutschen Nationalbibliothek:
Die Deutsche Nationalbibliothek verzeichnet diese Publikation in der Deutschen Nationalbibliografie;
detaillierte bibliografische Daten sind im Internet über http://dnb.dnb.de abrufbar.

© 2017 Dar al Janub – Verein für antirassistische und friedenspolitische Initiative

Herstellung und Verlag: BoD – Books on Demand, Norderstedt

ISBN: 978-3-7431-7978-3

"Yes, it would be worthwhile to study clinically, in detail,
the steps taken by Hitler and Hitlerism and to reveal to the very distinguished,
very humanistic, very Christian bourgeois of the twentieth century that without his being
aware of it, he has a Hitler inside him, that Hitler inhabits him,
that Hitler is his demon, that if he rails against him, he is being inconsistent and that,
at bottom, what he cannot forgive Hitler for is not crime in itself,
the crime against man, it is not the humiliation of man as such,
it is the crime against the white man, the humiliation of the white man,
and the fact that he applied to Europe colonialist procedures which until then had been
reserved exclusively for the Arabs of Algeria, the coolies of India, and the blacks of Africa."

Aimé Césaire

The three-day symposium "Remapping Palestine" in the autumn 2011 and the Club's internal debate of the content of the conference and the interventions against it - more by chance and luck - launched a new chapter in the work of the association, Dar al Janub.

The deepened critique of European and US-American money lending policy (the so called "development aid"), which emerged from the evaluation of "Remapping Palestine" that became a separate publication, lead to the internal decision to take new paths and to implement the critique in the Association's own modest practice.

The realization of a cooperative project in Palestine under the title "The Palestinian Women Economic & Cultural Empowerment Project in the Governorate of Nablus", funded by the OPEC Fund for International Development (OFID) should be seen as a direct result of the symposium and the focus of its discussion.

A special feature of the composition of the podium in 2011 was the fact that it was possible to bring together, at one table, Palestinians from all over the world, and thus to break through the prevalent exclusion of their voices in international and especially in European debates. Through the participation of anti-racist and anti-colonial Israeli dissidents, a unique atmosphere was created. It was neither one of these popular "normalization debates" in which European sponsors attempt to "network" Israeli and Palestinian representatives as equal discussion partners in utter disregard of the asymmetry of the conflict, nor a "peace negotiation". But it was a debate that was conducted based on the belief that the future can only be built in a free and just Palestine and with the involvement of all sections of Palestinian society - in western exile, in refugee camps and ghettos, those behind the wall, and in the blockaded Gaza strip.

Such a project, it seems, made the direct intervention of the Israeli embassy in Vienna inevitable as well as making the subsequent panic-stricken reaction of the Austrian Development Agency (ADA) comprehensible.[1] The forceful appearance of the Israeli ambassador in the premises of the ADA at that time clearly demonstrated how intransparent and ultimately anti-democratic the political process in West European countries actually is. It shows how little importance parliamentary majorities or boards and committees of the parliaments really have, when in the 200-year-old tradition of the Vienna Congress, decisions and resolutions are made by a selected few behind closed doors. This tradition of the Vienna Congress from 1815, which initiated the colonization of the Arabian region (planned among other things as an inter-European cooperation) is exemplary of the permanent exclusion of Palestinian voices in the debate about the future of Palestine. Just as in 1815, the only world power that was the subject of the negotiations, namely the slowly dying Ottoman Empire, was not invited to Vienna, today the Palestinian are treated similarly in the meetings of various Middle East Quartets and other such bodies.

In this context, the Palestinian Authority (PA) is not a legitimate representative of all Palestinians, nor does it currently seem to have any objectives and prospects for the implementation of a just peace solution for Palestine. The PAs dependence on Western funds and its deep involvement with the Israeli occupation authorities makes it an unreliable representative - even for the part of Palestinian society it can claim to represent. In 2014, in the wake of massive repression against Palestinians in the West Bank, and before the devastating attack on the Gaza Strip, Mahmoud Abbas showed his distance from the interests of the population by not terminating the security cooperation with Israel - a cooperation, which exclusively serves the interests of Israel.

The definitely positive impulse of our 2011 conference and the following evaluation concerning colonial domination under neo-liberal constraints (see the publication „Remapping Palestine: Entwicklung und Absicherung imperialer und neokolonialer Herrschaft am Beispiel Palästinas Teil 1", ISBN: 978-3732286713) resulted in two important initiatives:

REALIZING A COOPERATIVE PROJECT

A project promoted by the OPEC Fund for International Development (OFID) allowed our association to turn the more or less theoretical critique of NGO's, their growing role, and what is often called development policy in a colonial and neo-liberal context into practical steps in the form of a cooperative project in the West Bank. The prerequisites were long years of sounding out the Palestinian community and building trust with them. The critical evaluation of several western NGO projects had led to an important premise: before trying to realize an idea, a project, or a goal in such a politically and socially contested area, the right attitude is needed – humility - and the right partners. Given the relatively restricted influence and reputation we had in the field of cooperative development, it was surprising that our project was promoted by the OFID. Above all, because the project application included a sharp critique of NGO policy, and there was no objection from the OFID.

The granting of funds put us in the role of "Western donors", who would bear overall and responsibility for the project, which forced us to take off our "western glasses" and to look at and interpret the concrete needs of our partner SCCS in Nablus. It is one thing to recognize colonial hierarchies in theory, and to analyze and disentangle the paternalistic behavior of various western NGOs, but it is an entirely different thing to uncover your own privileged situation in the daily practical work, and particularly the attitude of "knowing it all better". We still cannot determine accurately if the project helped us more as Europeans, or if it helped the modest reconstruction of a Palestinian civil community yet more. One thing that must not remain unmentioned, which was already clear in 2011 and then confirmed at the conference in 2014, is the fact that NGOs and the phenomenon of NGOisation represent great problems for achieving a just and decolonized future for Palestine.

Old City Wall – Acre (Akko) 1936

Nevertheless, these phenomena are not the root of the problem, but rather the consequence of a colonial conquest entailed by the Oslo process. Even considering all the justified critiques of NGOs and the need to uncover their colonial functions, it is clear that the NGO system could only work because of the political conditions in 1990, and the agreements and objectives set out by Europe, the USA and Israel.

The so called Oslo Peace Process and the resulting "invasion" of western NGOs allowed an entire generation of Palestinian to grow up without knowledge of the period of the Intifada and their own history of self-organization and resistance. The occupation regime de facto (despite or even because of the Oslo agreements and the establishment of the PA) was continued seamlessly and actually expanded. The building of illegal settlements not only continued but also expanded beyond expectations. Nevertheless, the peace process achieved a rudimentary stabilization of the occupation besides numerous "side effects". The deeper analysis of this stabilization has to be done at some other point; only the essential points are listed here: the international isolation of Israel, especially in the global south, was reversed by the Oslo Process, and Israel was able to turn its former balance of payments deficit into a surplus. For instance, all aid payments for the benefit of Palestinian society, coming from NGOs and international lenders, have to first be exchanged from dollars or euros to shekels. Consequently, Israel's central bank receives great amounts of foreign currency.

In effect, Israel has found a way to export the occupation through the Oslo agreements. As a result, the occupation of Palestinian territory has become Israel's second largest export article – right after its weapons industry.

The stabilization of the occupation and the related "normalization" and NGOisation had profound implications for Palestinian society without bringing any improvement of living standards to the majority of the population. On the contrary, through the NGOisation it was possible to erode the collective experience of self-organization, and the resistance and solidarity of the Palestinian society to a certain degree.

The "reconstruction" of these collective experiences from the first Intifada can also be understood as a reacquisition of Palestinian history. Social work, as performed by autonomous institutions of Palestinian civil society (i.e. those independent of western donors) has very little to do with western "social work". Investments in "indestructible" infrastructure (education, training, "empowerment", charitable institutions) - instead of the destructible infrastructure preferred by Oslo-related investments - help independent and autonomous Palestinian organizations to maintain their resistance to the occupation. That is another reason why many of these committees and organizations have to work under repression and massive restrictions by western states.

THE BDS MOVEMENT

During the same period Palestinian civil society drew another important conclusion from its experiences with the Oslo process. In 2005, more than 170 Palestinian organizations signed the „Palestinian Call for Boycott, Divestment and Sanctions against Israel". In a mere 10 years, a worldwide BDS movement developed, which can no longer be ignored by the mainstream. This campaign has actively influenced the international discourse for years, and in 2014 a group was established in the hometown of Theodor Herzl in Austria - Israel's brutal military campaign in Gaza in that year was not the only reason. It is important to note at this point that several initiatives like "Women in Black (Vienna)" had for years included the BDS theme in their work, had emphasized networking – not least with Israeli dissidents - and still continue in this direction.

However, and this is not insignificant, there are alarming tendencies in the civil society campaigns of BDS. In some diplomatic notes BDS has already been indirectly referred to, for instance the US Secretary of State, John Kerry, facing the imminent collapse of the Middle East negotiations, threatened Israel with possible consequences, and used the term "boycott".

This embrace on the political level opens the door for positions that would like to channel the colonial project in Palestine into a reformable version that would leave the corner stones of the underlying Zionism untouched. Such developments strengthens forces inside the BDS movement, which regard the Palestinian Call of 2005 as the lowest common denominator - like a "special offer" in a supermarket, where you "buy" some things, and leaves others, such as "the right of return", sitting on the shelf.

Moreover, the attempted takeover of the BDS movement by the PA is questionable because BDS, as is a civil society campaign, must remain independent from governmental and semiofficial institutions. Among other developments with potentially serious consequences is the takeover of BDS positions by a small, elite western-trained group of Palestinians, who pursue their own interests, and present themselves as "natives". By skillful deployment of this "capital" they could gradually annul essential positions of the BDS movement.

THE "ONE-STATE-SOLUTION" DEBATE

The purely academic debate about the one-state-solution ("One-Democratic-State") is an example of this problem. This debate includes neither the representative of the Palestinians in Gaza, nor of the refugee camps or of the civil resistance. Moreover, the issue of the really existing "one-state" (i.e. Israeli control within and beyond the Green line) is not so much as mentioned. Ever since the Zionist pioneers began Jewish colonization in Palestine, Palestinians have been used as cheap labor in the manner of older colonialisms. In addition, traditional right-wing Zionism long wanted to integrate the native population in the Zionist project as a subordinate population.

For example, when the Palestinian political scientist Leila Farsakh who lives in the USA was asked what a binational State might look like, she replied: "It would be a parallel state structure, both the Israelis as well as the Palestinians would have to be recognized. The local governmental structure would remain intact, but there would be a common defense and foreign policy. Of course, for that to work, both sides would have to trust each other. The question is, how to create trust when so much violence characterized the past."[2]

Al Jazzar Mosque – Acre (Akko) 1936

With this she negates the close cooperation of the PA with Israel. This cooperation is of course based on the dependency created by Oslo, but this alone does not relieve the Palestinian Authority from responsibility. For instance, the local governmental structure of the PA allows it to track Palestinians who oppose Israel in the West Bank. Then at night, after the Palestinian security forces retreat, these individuals are arrested by the Israeli military. The contemplated common defense and foreign policy is most clearly visible in Gaza: after massive Israeli bombardments no support or help whatsoever reached Gaza on the part of the PA.

The BDS movement must be aware of the fallacy that BDS or some parliamentary majorities alone can achieve a just solution.

The pressure on Israel at this time can be measured by the amount of money it invests in lobby work to promote their image in the European parliaments. For instance, as research by David Cronin shows, the European Friends of Israel (EFI) had an estimated budget of €400.000 for the year 2012. This money is used to invite parliamentarians from Europe to Israel and the occupied territories to persuade them of the democratic nature of the regimes. However, it is not just the amount of money that is noteworthy about this lobbying; especially interesting is where the money comes from. One sponsor of the EFI is Israel Aircraft Industries, one of the biggest armaments manufacturers in Israel.

Just how distant from ethics or any moral concepts the invited parliamentarians often are can be seen in how openly they deal with contacts or invitations from the EFI. For example, a representative in the Austrian parliament, Petra Bayr (SPÖ), documented her participation at an EFI conference on her homepage without any concern. This demonstration of solidarity is especially relevant in view of the fact that this representative has been chairwoman of the "Subcommittee on Development Policy" of the parliament since 2003.

This example illustrates how little impact parliamentary decisions actually have in Europe. It is more-or-less irrelevant whether the Austrian parliament or a political party does or does not recognize the "State of Palestine" or whether the UN flies the Palestinian flag or not. As long as European politicians are manipulated by the Israeli armaments industry there will be no justice for Palestinians.

Sustainable development - one of the favorite terms of official development policy - is an empty phrase because it is not possible under the conditions of occupation and war. This holds true not only with respect to the repeated destruction of infrastructure that was financed with development money (i.e. airports, casinos, water treatment and power generating facilities, etc.), but also for the entire Palestinian economy and society. If projects in international development cooperation, including those supported by the Austrian Development Agency, are to be taken seriously, they would have to have the goal of empowering the population to shake off the occupation. Under conditions of continuing occupation and economic strangulation, western development aid not only turns Palestinians into supplicants and beggars, it is also used to implant western ideology and values. In typical colonial manner, Palestinians are denied their own history (e.g. by totally ignoring the lively women's rights movement in Palestine, which began long before and continued throughout the Intifada), to portray it as inferior and underdeveloped with the ultimate goal of breaking the resistance.

The publication at hand is a report on a two-year project, "The Palestinian Women's Economic & Cultural Empowerment's Project in the Governorate of Nablus" which we, as an association for antiracism and peaceful political initiatives, initiated in a modest attempt to implement the above-mentioned criticism in our daily work.

[1] In the beginning of May 2011, after careful examination of the application for a subsidy, the ADA granted and reserved Euro 7000 from their budget for the conference. Dar al Janub was informed by E-Mail, and in mid-July a contract was signed. By mid-August flights and rooms for invited speakers had been booked, posters and materials for distribution at the conference printed, and the organizers began to make public announcements and to send out invitations. Three days after the first announcement in our newsletter, various newspaper articles critical of the conference began to appear. On the 6th of September 2011 – six weeks before the conference – our Association received a letter from the head of the "Department for the Promotion of Civil Society" of the ADA to inform us that "it was not possible for the ADA to provide financial support for the project." For further details see: http://www.dar-al-janub.net/index.htm

[2] http://derstandard.at/2000010912555/Politologin-Projekt-eines-palaestinensischen-Nationalstaats-ist-gescheitert

ECONOMIC AND CULTURAL EMPOWERMENT
OF PALESTINIAN WOMEN IN THE GOVERNORATE OF NABLUS

THE GENESIS OF AN IDEA

The idea for this project resulted from several visits to Palestine by Dar al Janub activists that took place between 2006 and 2011. One of the most obvious impressions of these trips was, one hand, the omnipresence of Western "aid" and "development" organizations and, on the other, especially in the West Bank, the poor and increasingly precarious social and economic conditions of the Palestinian people. A closer look, however, revealed the structure, objectives, and policy of a Western-supported "development industry".

Moreover, we were confronted by the hard struggle for survival of local Palestinian welfare and social institutions, which received no funding from Western donors because they were considered "Islamic". Just like the Israeli occupying power, Western donors seemed to dislike the objectives and grass-root social initiatives of local organizations because these aspired to an independent Palestinian economy. Their struggle for autonomy, and self-management and empowerment is an alter-native to the policy of dependence that was implemented during the Oslo-period. It appears that from a Western perspective this makes these local NGO's ineligible for support.

This alarming situation was the basis of discussions between "The Social Charitable Center Society" (SCCS) and Dar al Janub, which resulted in the idea of the development-project "We are Nablus". Taking into account that Palestinian initiatives are constrained by the occupation and that "empowerment" without "power" may not be sustainable, the members of both organizations formulated the guiding principles for a project in the rebuilt old town of Nablus. Projects that "normalize" the occupation will not be able to achieve sustainability. Such a goal can only be realized by strengthening local, autonomous structures of the Palestinian people.

For SCCS and Dar al Janub such an approach required a true equality in their cooperation, which means that there is not one side that brings development and the other that receives the help. Any alert visitor to Nablus will see the benefits that millennia of human development have brought about, so it would be far more than presumptuous to call this project "development" cooperation. Nablus is a lively and functioning city. Although it is in a permanent state of emergency, has high unemployment and little chance of re-establishing the old small-scale industries, it is a perfect example of organizing a way of living under these harsh circumstances. Therefore, it represents a grand opportunity to learn about self-organization, especially for development projects in the Western part of the world. In Nablus, "development" is not a matter of "development by Western donors"; it is rather a matter of recognizing and overcoming the obstacles that inhibit self-development, which were put in place by the occupation and the Western world.

PROJECT BACKGROUND

Palestinian women make up approximately half of Palestinian society. An analysis of the Palestinian legislative elections in 2006 revealed that Palestinian women were involved widely in political action and public affairs. The ratio of women who participated in the elections was 47% (versus 53% for men); 44% of these women voted in favor of the opposition. The latter came from the young, poor and marginalized parts of society, and consequently, their votes must be regarded as a clear statement for change. They testify to a readiness to find alternatives for confronting the continuing state of war and occupation. The achievement of sustainable development presupposes that women, especial-ly those from marginalized parts of the society, participate in the development of ways to resist the occupation and to defend the rights of the Palestinian people.

There is a very urgent need for the establishment of an effective Palestinian national economy. Today, 75% of this economy depends on Israel. This fact is compounded by Israel's control over most of the land through confiscation, the apartheid wall, and the "closure of areas" policy. These factors work against the expansion of the Palestinian economy. Moreover, the structural distortions of the Palestinian economy are exacerbated by the policies of donors and funding countries. These policies increase economic dependence and undermine the efforts to establish a sustainable national economy that would benefit all sectors of the Palestinian people. Independent NGOs and grass-roots movements in both Gaza and the West Bank, who represent large parts of the young, poor and marginalized social segments, lost their economic base after the international isolation of the Gaza Strip by western donors, and Israel's blockade and attack.

As a result of Oslo and the blockade following the elections in 2006, class contradictions reached their peak. Women who supported the Islamic orientation, and rejected the policy of the Oslo Accords, suffered the most because the rate of women's participation in the production process is no higher than 15%, compared to 67% for men.

In addition, the unemployment rate in occupied Palestine is around 30%, and more than 50% of the female workforce is out of work, most of whom are university graduates. Western funded projects and institutions (of the Palestinian Authority as well as civil society) were subjected to a policy of excluding or marginalizing the political and social forces, especially women, who rejected Western domination. This exclusion policy was confirmed by the words of a Palestinian minister, who said that the dismissal of many of the staff in the ministries was based on their political backgrounds. Interestingly, this minister was the director of a non-governmental human right organization funded by the USA!

Women at the Well – Hebron (Al Khalil) 1935

I. ISSUES AND PROBLEMS

1. It is evident that, especially among younger members of Palestinian society, unemployment increased dramatically in the preceding years. Women are most affected by such developments.

2. The Oslo peace process put in place a donor policy that sharpened the internal contradictions of Palestinian society by creating and supporting social elites. As a result, Oslo failed to make sustainable development possible.

3. The aid and Western funding also shaped Palestinian civil society in a way that favored supposedly superior Western values such as individualism and personal autonomy over collectivism and self-sacrifice for collective activism. This policy, caused the shutdown of many traditional NGOS, and deprived large segments of the Palestinian people of the assistance of social services. Particularly affected, were social services for marginalized parts of the society such as women and the poor. Thus, what at first glance seems to be a conflict between Western and non-Western, or religious and secular values, turns out to be a class conflict between an impoverished part of the population and the elites (newly strengthened by the influx of donor money), as well as a contradiction between occupation and self-governance. Moreover, Western funding and assistance is bound to be temporary.

4. Consequently, building an independent economy and sustainable development is the key to making it possible for Palestinians to live in their land, and to resist an occupation that is based on land confiscation and the creation of Israeli settlements. This also requires the re-building of social structures that enabled the political participation of important parts of Palestinian society - with women at the very forefront. As already noted, these collective structures were undermined and partly destroyed by the NGOisation that was part of the Oslo process.

5. According to all indicators, the solution to the Israeli-Palestinian conflict is not near. Israel and its allies are trying to impose a state with uncertain borders, and to simultaneously promote the continuing fragmentation of the West Bank. To counteract these developments two goals must be aimed for:

- The creation of an independent Palestinian economy, based on its own capacities, which will allow as high a standard of living as possible.

- Building awareness and an intensified dialogue with opinion leaders and civil society representatives in Europe to enable them to understand the reality on the ground and the impacts and influences of Western private and official development aid.

6. The stereotypical perception and representation of Palestinian women as oppressed and passive, impedes the creation of the conditions for a dialogue among equals. This one-sided perception of Palestinian women reinforces prejudices on all sides. Young, poor, and marginalized Palestinian women have not been adequately and appropriately presented to and understood by the Western public.

II. BACKGROUND ON THE REGION

Since the Oslo Agreements, the social and economic situation in the West Bank and Gaza has worsened dramatically. De facto, the establishment of the so-called "Palestinian Authority" shifted the responsibility for satisfying the basic needs of the Palestinian population from the Israeli occupation authorities to the international community. This economic decline went hand in hand with an increase of Israeli settlements and the expropriation of Palestinian land. Under these conditions, the international community tried to strengthen the Palestinian infrastructure by building huge projects such as the international airport in Gaza and water processing facilities. In the meantime, most of these facilities and infrastructure improvements were destroyed by Israeli acts of war and aggression.

Since the Gaza war in 2008-2009, the economic situation there has continued to worsen dramatically, and in the West Bank small industries and agriculture that were formerly intact do not exist anymore. Only a small number of such enterprises remain and provide incomes to just a small minority of people. It is not surprising therefore that many Palestinians perceive themselves as people that have been reduced to asking international donors for handouts. Unemployment, unclear political prospects, and the ongoing military pressure have had enormously destructive effects on Palestinian society. Certainly, humanitarian help from international donors is needed, but it should be understood that this help is neither sustainable, nor can it bring about a long-term solution of the Israeli-Palestinian conflict.

Western donors invested large amounts of money in the training and equipment of police forces in the West Bank. This kind of donor policy gives the impression of a very selective assistance that aims to keep an occupied society under control. Yet, at the same time, this selective support widens the economic gap in the West Bank: privileged regions (e.g. Ramallah) and elite groups profit from the money of Western donors, but the majority of people (most of them in Area C) do not have any economic benefit.

In recent years, numerous Palestinian NGOs that were dependent on international donations had to close because the Palestinian Authority or international institutions cut financial support based on false grounds, i.e. claiming that these NGOs supported terrorism. As a result, the traditional, faith-based "Zakat Committees" became of great social relevance. Without them or other self-organized neighborly help, the situation would be even worse. These committees organize medical treatment, books for schools, building material for destroyed houses and so on.

In addition, Zakat Committees provide the means to implement sustainable activities in the areas of education, social work and economic development.

The beneficiaries of these services, instead of "receiving help", become an active part of the Committees, thereby making it possible for others to help themselves. For example: Women working in cooperatives can make their families more independent from Western donors and can build sustainable economic prospects. Young people, who can get a proper education in safe places, can develop perspectives with fewer worries about war and occupation, and will be able to pass on the concept of "education against oppression" to others.

On the international plane, the creation of a Palestinian state has receded into the distance. From the perspective of Palestinian civil society, however, it is very important to organize life and to develop alternatives to the ongoing state of war and occupation.

In spite of numerous initiatives (Roadmap, Geneva Initiative, etc.) no solution is in sight, but a just solution for Israelis and Palestinians still is a central aspect of peace for the whole Middle-East region. The European Union is a very important player in this respect. But although, on the one hand, it is accepted as independent and objective, on the other, it is not active or willing enough to play an effective role in supporting Palestinian rights.

There is a lack of knowledge in Europe about the historical, political and social background, and about the institutions of Palestinian civil society. Consequently, opinions about Palestinian culture and society are often shaped by prejudices. Moreover, the legitimate rights of Palestinians are not represented adequately. NGOs that have an Islamic background are boycotted because their work is perceived as not being in line with "Western values". However, unless all different parts of the Palestinian society are included, - especially NGOs, politicians, and scientists with an Islamic cultural and religious background - Palestinian society will not be able to achieve a peaceful and sustainable state.

III.   GENERAL OBJECTIVES

1. Improving the leadership capacities of Palestinian women. Education should enable women to strengthen their role within Palestinians society, help defend Palestinian rights against occupation, empower women to articulate their agendas vis-a-vis Western donors, and foster dialogue with European civil society.

2. Helping to achieve a sustainable economic future by creating jobs and incomes for women in the occupied territories.

3. Empowering local communities to become more independent from Western donors and the Israeli economy.

4. Raising awareness of and increasing sensitivity to the specific nature of development in Palestine

5. Changing the prevailing public opinion in Europe that Palestinian women are oppressed by and dependent on Palestinian men.

6. Enhancing the dialogue between Austrian and Palestinian civil society

IV. SPECIFIC OBJECTIVES

1. Providing financial support for sustainable projects such as folk embroidery, natural soap production, and glass painting. These projects will be supervised and carried out by Palestinian women. The products will be destined for sale in Western, as well as local and regional markets.

2. Eliminating the stereotypes and prejudices, which assert that women's adherence to their Palestinian, Muslim culture and civilization poses a threat to the West, by showing the diverse aspects and faces of Palestinian civil society.

3. Promoting visits and meetings between Palestinian Muslim women leaders and Western leaders to create dialogue, interaction and cooperation through the exchange of views on political, economic, social, and cultural aspects of Palestinian society.

4. Providing the opportunity for Palestinian women leaders to visit the West to explain the situation in Nablus from their perspective and to deliver insights into the actual political, economic and human-rights situation in Palestine.

5. Promoting exchange visits that can serve as a communication platform between Western and Palestinian NGOs.

6. Establishing empowerment training for marginalized Palestinian women in the governorate of Nablus to improve their economic, political and legal opportunities and to increase their participation in public life.

7. Holding exhibitions of Palestinian products locally, regionally, and internationally.

8. Creating a showroom for displaying and selling products of the Nablus project. In the long term, the project will be financed with those revenues.

9. Establishing markets for Palestinian products in Europe.

10. Presenting the political, social and humanitarian situation of Palestinian society to the European public.

V. PROPOSED ACTIVITIES

1. Promoting increased production of regional products such as natural soaps, all types of folk embroidery, and glass-painting. This will foster local capacities and the skills of marginalized women in Nablus.

2. Conducting feasibility studies for this kind of local projects and for exporting the proposed products.

3. Preparing materials and training manuals for the projects.

4. Holding workshops and training courses for women who will engage in these projects.

5. Preparing training materials for civic education, human rights, and international humanitarian law.

6. Conducting training sessions, lectures, workshops, and meetings for Palestinian women to train them in the issues mentioned above. Participants should become aware of their right to resist the occupation.

7. Organizing meetings between the leaders of the participating Palestinian women and representatives of Western opinion-makers.

8. Providing showrooms to exhibit and sell the products of the project and using the proceeds to expand the project. As already mentioned, the project should increasingly become self-financing.

9. Training of 200 women in matters related to civic education, administration, economy, human rights, and law. Three four-month courses, each with 66 participants, will be conducted.

VI. BENEFICIARIES

Direct Beneficiaries

- A group of 15 to 30 marginalized and unemployed women with qualifications and scientific skills to participate in and supervise the above-mentioned economic projects.

- A group of 200 girls, between the ages of 18 and 40, will be selected on the basis of being marginalized politically and economically.

- A group of 15 to 30 Austrian students and academics that are engaged in the project and the resulting dialogue.

Indirect beneficiaries

- Marginalized and unemployed women who benefit from the economic outcome of the project (300 estimated).

- Women who benefit from the conferences and public events (500 estimated).

- Family and community members of Nablus who benefit from the economic outcome and the improved capacities of the women participating in the project (700 estimated).

- Austrian students and academics that benefit from public events in Austria (700 estimated).

VII.   THE IMPLEMENTING NGOS

The Social Charitable Center Society (Nablus)

The Social Charitable Center Society (SCCS) was established in 1978 in the city of Nablus, which is the second largest city of the West Bank. It is a nonprofit, nongovernmental organization. It was founded by a group of people to provide support, and humanitarian and social services to the poor and needy. The SCCS focuses also on providing support to the injured and marginalized women and children of the city. The SCCS was established in the old city center of Nablus, where the poorest people live.

SCCS provides health, social, educational, cultural, and rehabilitation services to women and children who suffer from certain health problems. In addition, SCCS also runs a kindergarten for children under the age of six, and offers professional childcare for a very small, symbolic fee. The SCCS strives to expand its scope of community work for marginalized groups, especially women, through the implementation of cultural, social and economic projects.

The SCCS is registered and cooperates with the local authorities. It has an accurate and transparent accounting system, overseen by an external auditor who submits periodical reports.

The SCCS Board of Trustees sets policies for the Association and oversees its implementation. The Director General is responsible for presenting periodic reviews on work progress to the Board of Trustees.

Contact:

Social Charitable Center Society
Nablus, West Bank, Palestine
Tel./ Fax: +970 9 2384131
Website: www.sccs.ps
E-mail: sccs.nps@gmail.com

Dar al Janub – Union for
Antiracism and Peace Policy (Vienna)

Austrian, Turkish and Arab students founded the Austrian NGO, Dar al Janub, in November 2003. Its main goal is to raise awareness about developments in the Global South. Dar al Janub's activities focus mainly on issues concerning the Arab world, paying special attention to the humanitarian and political reality in Palestine. The goal is to improve the relations between Europe and the Arab world by analyzing and criticizing the colonial attitude of Europe.

To improve relations it is essential to overcome the historical cleavage between these regions and to create an atmosphere for a dialogue among equals. This requires bringing authentic Palestinian viewpoints to Europeans. The current problematic attitudes in Europe arise from a number of factors: a lack of understanding of the background of, and the reasons for the conflict in Palestine; the insensitivity of the public due to biased and fragmentary reporting; and the medias' downplaying of the fate of the Palestinian people, especially the Palestinian refugees.

Dar al Janub's main field of work is to fill this gap in the consciousness of European society. Developments in Palestine strongly influence the work with which we hope to make a contribution to ensuring the legitimate rights of the Palestinians, especially the right to an independent state and the Palestinian refugees' right of return.

Contact:

Dar al Janub –
Union for Antiracism and Peace Policy
Kleistgasse 8/3
1030 Vienna
Austria
Tel.: +43 (0) 676 78 93 413
Website: www.dar-al-janub.net
E-mail: union@dar-al-janub.net

VIII.   BUDGET

USD 100,000

IX. PERIOD OF TIME

24 month (01/01/2013 – 31/12/2014)

X. FUNDING ORGANIZATION

The OPEC Fund for
International Development

DATES, FACTS AND HISTORY OF NABLUS

- More than 145,000 inhabitants (with the refugee camps and villages 300,000 inhabitants)
- Second largest city of Palestine
- Founded 72 CE
- Surrounded by more than 10 illegal Israeli settlements
- Location: 42 kilometers east of Jaffa, 110 kilometers west of Amman, 63 kilometers north of al-Quds
- The University of Nablus (an-Najah) has more than 20,000 Students and was founded in 1977

- <u>History:</u>
- For 500 Years Nablus was a central trading center in the region, till the occupation
- Nablus had developed trade relations with Damascus, Cairo, Aleppo, Baghdad, Mosul and the Mediterranean Region
- In 1882, 32 soap factories were founded
- Nablus was the greatest producer of cotton in the region 225.000 k in the 1837
- The famous sweet Kunafeh has its origin in Nablus

- <u>History under Occupation:</u>
- In 2002 the Israeli army killed 80 people in the "Operation Defense Shield" in Nablus
- From June till September 2002 the Israeli army entered Nablus and imposed a 24 hour curfew in the so called "Operation Determined Path"
- Several mosques and the Greek Orthodox Church were damaged in these attacks
- In the old market, F-16 bombings destroyed 3 soap factories and created an overall loss of USD 80,000,000

AN ECONOMY UNDER OCCUPATION AND APARTHEID

THE EROSION OF THE PALESTINIAN ECONOMY BY THE OSLO PROCESS;
THE POLITICAL INFLUENCE OF "DEVELOPMENT PROGRAMS"

Abdul-Jabbar Khalili

An-Najah National University / SCCS

THE WEST BANK AND GAZA STRIP PRIOR TO THE FIRST INTIFADA, 1987

Frustration grew among the Palestinians in the Israeli-occupied West Bank and Gaza Strip in the 1980s following years of repression, extrajudicial killings, mass detentions, house demolitions, forced migrations, relocations and deportations. This Israeli "Iron Fist" policy against the Palestinian nationalism, among other causes, culminated in the outbreak of the first Intifada in 1987.

According to the Israeli human rights NGO, B'Tselem, between the beginning of the occupation in 1967 and the outbreak of the first Intifada in 1987, Israeli settlers, encouraged and guarded by military forces, confiscated about 42% of the total land of the West Bank (2,480,000 acres out of the 5.5 million total). They built approximately 185 different settlements (national religious, Ultra-Orthodox, secular, "military", etc.) to accommodate around 60,000 settlers until 1987. This number rose to 429,160 in 2003, 541,000 in 2012 and 580,801 settlers in 2013 living in about 503 settlements.

In the same period (1967-1987), settlers and military forces confiscated about 160 square kilometers out of the 363 square kilometers (42%) total area of the Gaza Strip. On this land, they built 31 settlements for about 12,000 settlers, who also consumed most of the water resources of the Gaza Strip.

The agricultural sector also suffered from the Israeli policies towards Palestinian farmers and their lands. In addition to the confiscation of land to build settlements, more lands (including arable lands) were confiscated for roads restricted to settlers, which at times prevented Palestinian farmers from reaching their own lands. The same occurred for so-called security reasons, which also resulted in the destruction of about 0.5 million trees, most of them ancient olive trees, between 1967 and 1987.

These measures against the Palestinians, especially the farmers, forced them to abandon their lands and become workers in newly-established Israeli farms, which were sometimes located on the confiscated lands in the West Bank and the Gaza Strip.

Women at the Well – Jericho (Ariha) 1945

On the eve of the first Intifada in 1987, the number of such workers was estimated to be about 109,000 (39.3% of the Palestinian work force). Palestinians were recruited mainly to do unskilled or semi-skilled jobs that Israelis did not want. These Palestinians were considered inferior and were made to work in hard conditions. In the context of Israeli restrictions on the Palestinian economy, these were clear manifestations of an apartheid policy. Moreover, Israel opened its labor market to workers from the occupied territories in 1972, thereby draining workers and skills from the Palestinian economy and making it dependent on Israel.

THE INTIFADA (1987)

The first Intifada was a protest against Israeli policies, against harassment, and against the military occupation in general. It is the natural response of a population, which was deprived of its fundamental rights and freedoms. It broke out in December 1987 and lasted until the Madrid Conference in 1991, though some date its end to the signing of the Oslo I Accord in 1993.

During these years, the Israeli military authority along with the settlers (encouraged and guarded by soldiers) committed all forms of repression in the West Bank and Gaza Strip including:

- Killings, physical violence and injuries – shootings, beatings, indiscriminate use of teargas;
- Settler violence;
- Arbitrary arrest and detention – administrative arrest, mass arrests, interrogation and torture, deaths in detention;
- Deportations;
- Collective punishment – house demolitions, curfews, and closed areas;
- Economic repression;
- Destruction of social institutions;
- Repression of freedom of information – press closures, harassment of journalists and human rights workers; and
- Deprivation of justice.

As far as the economic situation is concerned, the Israeli authorities made all efforts to strike down Palestinian attempts towards economic independence. Palestinians were called upon by the Intifada's united leadership to boycott Israeli goods as much as possible, resist taxes, and stop working in Israel as much as could be reasonably managed. Commercial strike days were orchestrated with remarkable levels of compliance. Home industries and measures of self-sufficiency (such as vegetable gardening) were encouraged to reduce dependency on Israeli produce. Each of these measures was met with severe counter-measures from the Israeli "civil" administration and armed forces.

Curfews and area closures set up siege conditions in an Israeli attempt to undermine Palestinian control of their own economic conditions. New limitations were placed on exports; the amount of money that could be brought into the West Bank and Gaza Strip was drastically reduced (JD 2000 – US$ 6000 and then to JD 400 – US$ 1200), and strong measures were taken against the population in attempts to break tax resistance. Other measures denied factories and small industries permits to expand, licenses to import/export, and the ability to obtain raw materials. Such measures, along with absenteeism due to curfews, closures, and strikes affected family incomes drastically.

THE OSLO ACCORDS

The Oslo I Accord, signed in 1993 and Oslo II Accord, signed in 1995, marked the first time that the State of Israel and the Palestine Liberation Organization (PLO) formally recognized one another, and publicly committed to negotiate a solution to their decades-long conflict based on territorial compromise.

The accords did not stipulate, but implied, the creation of a Palestinian state alongside Israel. That two-state vision required Israel to abandon its negation of Palestinian claims to national sovereignty, and Palestinians to accept that such claims would be limited to only a small part of the entire territory of historic Palestine for which the PLO had been fighting, recognizing Israel's sovereignty over the remainder.

The Oslo Accords were not a peace treaty, however. Instead, they established interim governance arrangements and a framework to facilitate negotiations for a final treaty, which would be concluded by the end of 1998.

Oslo transferred control of the major Palestinian cities in the West Bank and Gaza Strip from the Israeli military to a newly created Palestinian Authority. The hope was that limited Palestinian self-government and incremental Israeli withdrawal would boost mutual trust that would empower leaders on both sides to negotiate final-status agreements on the thorniest issues -- including Jerusalem, the fate of Palestinian refugees and Israeli settlements, and borders and security. To achieve that end, both parties participated in:

- The Gaza-Jericho Agreement, May 4, 1994;
- Interim Agreement on West Bank and Gaza Strip (Oslo II), September 28, 1995;
- Hebron Accord, January 15, 1997;
- Wye River Memorandum, October 15-23, 1998;
- Sharm El-Sheik Memorandum, September 4, 1999;
- Camp David Summit, July 11-25, 2000;
- The Taba Talks, January 21-27, 2007.

One crucial station in this thorny path was

- The Paris Protocol (or The Paris Economic Agreement), as part of the Gaza-Jericho Agreement to regulate the economic relations between them in four areas:
  - Labor,
  - Trade relations,
  - Fiscal issues and,
  - Monetary arrangements.

"SINGAPORE OF THE MIDDLE EAST"

In an attempt to market the Oslo Accords and to justify the marathon negotiations and discussions, the slogan "Singapore of the Middle East" was introduced first by the then Israeli foreign minister, Shimon Perez, and soon was repeated by negotiators and politicians on both sides. It was simply to say that after implementing the accords and agreements, the Middle East region, and the Palestinian territories, in particular, would enjoy prosperity and would become the "Singapore" of the Middle East.

To the Palestinians' dismay, this new "Singapore" was never born. Many obstacles were laid in the already thorny path of the peace process. More land was confiscated for settlements and for building roads for settlements, more violence from settlers was practiced, more orders to restrict the Palestinians' movements, and then came the separation or "apartheid" wall that divided the West Bank into "cantons and Bantustans." The promised prosperity vanished, and a new cycle of violence and repression, the second Intifada, started in 2000.

APARTHEID AND
THE SEPARATION WALL

The term "apartheid" is simply defined by the "Merriam Webster Dictionary" as:

"apart·heid: a former social system in South Africa in which black people and people from other racial groups did not have the same political and economic rights as white people and were forced to live separately from white people."

Obviously, this definition states that the apartheid policy appears when two parties / groups / or peoples are living together, but do not enjoy the same POLITICAL and ECONOMIC rights.

Does this apply to the Palestinian case? In fact, treating Palestinians as inferior to Jews and depriving them of their rights started decades earlier - before the construction of the Separation Wall that isolated the Palestinians in cantons and Bantustans. Actually, this segregation policy dated back to the early days of occupation in 1967, or rather, back to 1948 when the Zionists expelled the Palestinians and declared the establishment of the State of Israel on Palestinian land. This apartheid policy is exemplified by the following:

- In 1948-49, about 770,000 Palestinians were expelled (for the most part forcibly) from their homeland to make room for Jewish settlers in Palestine.

- After 1967, another 350,000 Palestinians were displaced (later, some of them were allowed to return).

- Palestinian villages in the Jerusalem area and elsewhere were immediately destroyed to build settlements for the Jews.

- Later, Palestinian homes, which were in the way of settlement expansion or other Israeli development projects, were demolished. Thousands of Palestinian homes have been demolished since 1967.

- Laws were enacted that forbade the Palestinians the right of return.

- Israeli citizens (including those living in the occupied and confiscated lands) have been subject to Israeli civil laws, and not the military law that governs the Palestinians.

- Thousands of landless Palestinians, absorbed into the Israeli economy as cheap, unskilled or semi-skilled laborers to work in jobs that Israelis shun, are paid substantially lower wages than Israelis with the same jobs, and do not receive worker benefits and medical services like their Jewish counterparts, although they are taxed at the same level as Israeli workers.

- Restrictions have been placed on Palestinian farmers who have been denied their own water, and who have not been allowed to grow, sell, and export certain kinds and amounts of crops - thus transforming the occupied territories into the Israel's largest export market.

- Restrictions are also placed on economic development. Business licenses for importation of machinery and production materials are delayed and are often denied. Limitations on exports are also practiced to serve the needs of the Israeli economy.

These practices continued even during the transitional phase after the signing of the Oslo Accords. Then, the separation wall was built, which emphasizes segregation, although security was the reason announced for building it.

In 2002, the government of Israel decided to construct a wall with the purported aim of preventing violent attacks by Palestinian militants inside Israel. However, the vast majority of the wall's route is located within the West Bank, rather than on the internationally recognized 1949 Armistice Line (Green Line). The wall is an integral part of a multi-layered system of physical and administrative obstacles that severely restrict Palestinian movement and access throughout the West Bank. It has worsened the fragmentation of the occupied Palestinian territories, compounded the increasing isolation of East Jerusalem from the rest of the territory, cut off land and access to resources that are needed for Palestinian development, and continues to undermine agricultural and rural livelihoods throughout the West Bank.

An estimated 62 per cent of the wall is complete, 10 per cent is under construction, and 28 per cent is planned but not yet built (as of 2014). In recent years, the construction of new parts has almost completely halted.
However, the negative humanitarian impact of the wall on Palestinian communities continues:

- Around 11,000 Palestinians living in 32 communities located between the wall and the Green Line depend on the granting of permits or special arrangements to continue to live in their own homes.

- Approximately 150 communities have land located behind the wall, forcing residents to apply for special permits or prior coordination to access this area. The agricultural livelihoods of thousands of families have been undermined due to the permit and gate regime, which restricts access to farmland behind the wall.

- The wall has reduced the access to work-places and essential services of Palestinians living in communities located behind the wall.

- The wall also adversely affects the West Banks urban centers, in particular, East Jerusalem where Palestinian neighborhoods and suburbs are separated from each other and walled out from the urban center.

Facts on the Wall: Upon Completion	
Projected Length of Wall:	832 km, more than double the length of the Green Line.
Location of Wall:	Only 6% of the wall will be within 100 meters of the Green Line.
Projected Land to be de facto Annexed into Israel:	11.9% of the Occupied West Bank
Projected Percentage of Settlers Outside Wall:	88.6%
Projected Percentage of Palestinians surrounded and isolated by the Wall:	89.5%
Number of Palestinians Isolated Between the Wall and the Green Line:	249,000 (10.5% of the Palestinian West Bank population). Of this, approximately 20,000 Palestinians will be living in the "closed zone."
Number of Palestinians who will be Separated from their Land by the Wall:	329,000 (13.8% of the Palestinian West Bank population)

On 9 July 2004, the International Court of Justice (ICJ) issued an "Advisory Opinion on the Legal Consequences of the Construction of a Wall in the Occupied Palestinian Territory." The ICJ stated that the sections of the wall route, which ran inside the West Bank, including East Jerusalem, violated Israel's obligations under international law. <u>The ICJ called on Israel to cease construction of the wall including in and around East Jerusalem and dismantle the sections already completed.</u> The Court also obligated member states not to recognize the illegal situation created by the barrier and to ensure Israel's compliance with international law.

The 9th of July 2014 marks 10 years since the ICJ's Advisory Opinion, but contrary to the recommendations of the Court, <u>very little has changed on the ground</u>. The wall continues to obstruct the movement of Palestinians as well as severely impacting their development and livelihood opportunities.

THE POLITICAL INFLUENCE OF "DEVELOPMENT PROGRAMS"

The 1967 war and the occupation of the West Bank and the Gaza Strip, previously controlled by Jordan and Egypt respectively, left a gap in social services, which many civil, local, and international institutions and organizations rushed to fill. The Zakat (charity) and the Red Crescent committees, in addition to UNRWA and other UN organizations, were among the first bodies that provided humanitarian aid to people. In addition, because of the large-scale disaster that resulted from the expulsion and dislocation of hundreds of thousands of people, other NGOs, both Palestinian and international, appeared on the scene and started providing aid and carrying out some development projects. The donors, then, were mainly the West and Arab States.

More and more civil organizations were founded in the 1980s to meet the increasing needs of the people. The number of these organizations sky-rocketed during the years of Intifada (1987 – 1993) to cope with the rapidly deteriorating situation. Some of the most active committees during the Intifada were the "Popular Committees", which were mostly run and supervised by different political factions. After the Oslo accords and the emergence of the Palestinian Authority (PA), many of the already existing NGOs were absorbed in the newly born PA ministries, while new organizations arose to fill the gaps that were left. Nevertheless, the main sources of aid continued to be Palestinian, and international, mainly from the West and the Arab States.

This humanitarian aid effectively financed a series of programs in the sectors of agriculture, infrastructure, housing, and education. The Western donors had two major goals: to fuel Palestinian economic growth and to build public support for the peace process and the negotiations with Israel. In a report for the Middle East Monitor in September 2013, Dr. Sarah Marusek wrote that "the foreign aid to

Palestinians existed only to support the 'peace process' industry." Therefore, humanitarian aid fluctuated in the late 1990s, and whenever the peace process lost momentum, the donors rushed to fuel it. James Wolfensohn, the president of the World Bank once said: "The sense of urgency is clear. Peace will only be assured in that area (the West Bank and Gaza Strip) if you can get jobs for those people." On May 1st 2006, James Wolfensohn, criticizing the Quartet's decision to suspend western aid, resigned from his post.

Women at the Well – Nablus 1935

With the outbreak of the second Intifada in 2000, social and economic conditions worsened once again, and most of the donations went for emergency programs rather than for development.

In 2006, after Hamas won the elections and assumed power in the Gaza Strip, a dramatic change in donor policy occurred. The Quartet (the UN, EU, USA and Russia) announced in a statement on January 31, 2006 that "all members of the future Palestinian government must be committed to non-violence, recognition of Israel and acceptance of previous agreements and obligations, including the roadmap." These political conditions have remained valid ever since. They surfaced again in 2009 during the Sharm El-Sheikh conference when the donors pledged $4.5 billion for the reconstruction of Gaza following the Israeli attack in 2008-2009. They made another appearance at the Cairo conference for the reconstruction of Gaza on October 12, 2014 following the most recent attack in July-August 2014 when the donors insisted that "reconstruction be linked to the reinstatement of the 'full' authority of the Palestinian presidency and to the donors' political conditions." The donors' fulfillment of their pledges would remain contingent on the Pales-tine Liberation Organization's (PLO) continued commitment to negotiations as its sole strategy.

Recently, many international NGOs either adopt the policies of the countries they belong to, or are forced by their countries to abide by these policies when coordinating any humanitarian aid or development programs. USAID, for example, stipulates that the end beneficiary in any project should renounce "violence", and it refuses funding to build a school if it is named after a well-known leader or martyr renowned for his or her national position and struggle against the occupier.

Adnan Odeh

Project Manager SCCS

ABOUT THE SOCIAL
CHARITABLE CENTER SOCIETY (SCCS)

The SCCS was established in the old city of Nablus, where more than 50,000 poor, under-educated, and low-income citizens live. Its programs work towards reform of the economic, social, and civil aspects of the local government. They also aim to bring about sustainable human development by disseminating knowledge, increasing awareness of the rights of children, women and the poor, expanding general knowledge of civic education, and increasing the development of technical and pedagogical skills among marginalized groups in general.

The SCCS believes that development by empowering the poor, marginalized women and children through the enhancement of their abilities including making their voices heard requires starting at a grassroots level and following a bottom-up approach.

SCCS is focusing on the work on the ground and the implementation of projects in the old city of Nablus. It provides health, social, educational, cultural, and rehabilitation services to women and children who suffer from certain health problems, in addition to the establishment of a kindergarten, which children under the age of six can attend for a symbolic fee, and kitchens that provide healthy food for poor families and children suffering from anemia.

The SCCS seeks to expand the scope of its community work for marginalized groups, especially women, by implementing cultural, social, and economic projects. Throughout the years, SCCS has, by training poor and unemployed women, helped them find work and establish careers. There have been many success stories of women, who work in the fields of embroidery, knitting, cosmetic art and hairdressing. They became owners of profitable ventures. To reduce unemployment among young female university graduates, SCCS initiated tutoring courses for poor students. Two goals were achieved: improving the economic situation of young female teachers, and improving the educational status of poor students. Through this program, SCCS actively contributes to a reduction of illiteracy rates, school dropout rates, and early marriage. Education is the main factor in breaking the cycle of poverty. By all these means and through empowerment of marginal segments of the population SCCS resisted the occupation.

THE ECONOMIC SITUATION

Since the conclusion of the Oslo Accords, the economic and social situation in the West Bank and Gaza has worsened dramatically. The establishment of Palestinian "autonomy" implied that the Israeli occupation authorities passed on their responsibility for satisfying the basic needs of Palestinians to the international community. This economic deterioration went hand in hand with the increase of Israeli settlements and the expropriation of Palestinian land. In this situation, the international community tried to foster the Palestinian infrastructure by building huge projects such as an international airport in Gaza, industrial zones and water processing facilities.

However, most of these facilities and infrastructures were destroyed by Israel's acts of war and aggression - particularly in Gaza, where the economic situation has continued to deteriorate since 2009. In the West Bank, small industries and agricultural businesses, that were intact in former times, no longer exist. The small numbers of enterprises that remain provide income for just a few people.

Nablus is the main urban and commercial center and the second largest city in the West Bank. Its total population is 160,000, and the entire governorate (i.e. the Nablus administrative region) population is almost 370,000. The old city of Nablus, the location of the project, is an important place for traditional industries such as the production of soap, olive oil, sweets, sesame tahini, and handicrafts. The city is also a regional trading center for fresh produce.

Trade - either within the West Bank, or in form of exports to Israel or abroad - requires a free flow of goods, which cannot exist because the international borders are under full Israeli control and Nablus is surrounded by sixteen Israeli checkpoints and eleven settlements. The existence of settlements leads to violations of human rights, including the rights to property, equality, an adequate standard of living, and freedom of movement.

The Israeli government controls 45% of the West Bank territories, including the governorate of Nablus, which contains the second largest settlement bloc that amounts to 32% of all settlements in the occupied territories. In Nablus, 44.6% of the land has been declared to be "closed military zones" by Israeli military orders. These zones are off limits to Palestinians, except by special permit. In contrast, Israeli citizens, and tourists from anywhere in the world can freely enter these areas. In total, the settlements and the areas under the jurisdiction of the regional councils cover 63% of Area C (under full Israeli control) and Palestinians are prohibited from construction or development in these areas.

Why is Nablus, in particular, so strongly targeted? Because it is rich in water resources, has fertile agricultural land (as part of the Jordan valley), and has well-trained workers.

Harvest of Olives – Nablus 1935

85% of all Nablus' water resources are under Israeli control. The Palestinians can only obtain one third of what is available to Israelis - at three times the price. The West Bank settlements inhabited by around 600,000 settlers destroy the environment by producing 18 million cubic meters of wastewater yearly.

In the last eight years, the Israeli occupation authority destroyed 315 housing units in the Jordan valley, 1,600 people were displaced, including 658 children. During the past four years, 86 houses were destroyed in Nablus, leaving 358 people homeless including 142 children.

As a result of the Israeli confiscation of agricultural land, the high cost of water, and the destruction of wells and houses in the northern part of the Jordan valley, the total irrigated land available to Palestinians has decreased by 49%.

Since 1967, 800,000 olive trees have been up-rooted in the occupied territories resulting in a loss of around $55 million to the Palestinian economy, with Nablus being the most seriously affected. The olive sector contributes $100 million yearly to some of the poorest Palestinian communities. It is worth mentioning that the number of olive trees has decreased by 76%. In 1967, there were 500,000 olive trees, but now only 119,000 are left.

Palestinian industries have been seriously handicapped due to the above-mentioned factors, but also due to checkpoints and border restrictions that hinder transportation. As a result, production has declined in recent years. Many businesses have either moved or been established outside of Nablus, i.e. beyond the tight ring of closure around the city.

Before the Israeli occupation in 1967, more than 4,000 tons of the famous Nablus soap (made of olive oil) was produced, which constituted 67% of Nablus exports. By the year 2000, production had fallen to 600 tons, which constituted only 41.5% of all exports. After the Israeli invasion in 2002, the production declined again to only 300 tons, which then constituted a mere 36% of all exports.

In the 1960s and 1970s, 32 soap factories operated in Nablus, employing hundreds of people. Now only eight factories are still operational. In earlier times, Nablus had hundreds of match, shoe, and artisanal factories, but due to the tax system, price dumping, and the high cost of production most of them were ruined and had to close. Furthermore, during the 2002 Israeli invasion, three of the main historical soap factories and several bazaars (such as blacksmithing and onion markets) were demolished.

The Nablus Chamber of Commerce reports that considerable investment capital has moved from Nablus to the Ramallah governorates, and some to Jordan and still other countries. The loss of economic activity within the city has contributed to the increase of unemployment from 18.2% in 1999 to 26.3% in 2006. In 2014, the unemployment rate shot even higher, and was estimated to be 32% by the municipality of Nablus.

The shocking impact of the Israeli occupation on the Palestinian economy and society becomes apparent when it is understood that two decades after the Oslo Accords, an Israeli citizen's income is 15 times higher than that of a Palestinian's despite the fact that there is a unified customs system. In 1993, the per capita income of the Palestinians was $2,000, and only reached $2,093 by 2013. In contrast, the Israeli per capita income was $13,800 in 1993, and reached $32,000 in 2013.

The standard of living of the Palestinian population is steadily deteriorating. Despite high levels of international aid since the Oslo Accords were signed, the heavy Palestinian dependence on the Israeli economy, Israeli policies of territorial control, illegal settlement activity, roadblocks, and separation barriers have made it all but impossible for the West Bank and Nablus to flourish.

We should not be surprised therefore, that many Palestinians perceive themselves as people that have been degraded to the status of supplicants for international aid. Unemployment, the lack of political perspectives, settlements and the ongoing military pressure has had enormously destructive effects on Palestinian society. Indeed, humanitarian assistance by international donors is necessary, but this help is neither sustainable, nor will it contribute to a long-term solution of the Israeli-Palestinian conflict.

Western donors invested large amounts of money in training and equipment for selective recipients. Privileged regions, such as Ramallah, and elite groups, such as NGOs, benefit from the money of the Western donors. But the majority of the Palestinian people (most of them in Area C) are excluded from these economic benefits.

"Zakat Committees" are of great social relevance (see note on p. 44). Without these committees, or other self-organized neighborly help, the situation would be even worse.

These committees organize medical treatment, books for schools, building material for destroyed houses, etc.

Additionally, "Zakat Committees" provide the necessary means to implement sustainable activities for education, social work, and economic development. The beneficiaries of these services, instead of "just receiving help", become an active part of civil society. "Zakat Committees" thereby create the possibility for people to help themselves.

The need to establish an effective Palestinian national economy is very urgent. Today, 75% of the Palestinian economy depends on Israel. This problem has been compounded by Israel's control over most of the land and water by means of confiscation, the apartheid wall, and the "closure of areas" policy. These policies severely limit the possibility of enhancing Palestinian trade and labor standards.

The structural distortions in the Palestinian economy have also grown due to the policies of donors and funding countries. Such funding enforces economic dependence on others instead of supporting the establishment of a sustainable national economy that includes all sectors of the Palestinian people. Under the occupation Israeli authorities systematically disadvantaged, independent NGOs and grass-roots movements that represent large parts of the young, poor, and marginalized segments of the society.

SOCIAL CONDITIONS

The most dangerous impact that Israeli and international aid-oriented economic policies have had on Palestinian society is the steady decline of the middle class. Israel is targeting this sector because the presence of a strong middle class would play a significant positive role in economic growth and good governance. This would work to achieve a middle class consensus for economic development and social peace, and thereby minimize the confrontations between the poor and elites.

In addition, the middle class, in Palestine generally and in Nablus specifically, played a very important role in resisting the occupation. For instance, the 1936 revolution and the great six-month strike against British colonialism and Zionist immigration, began at a Nabulsi soap factory. And in the 1980's, after initial protests in Gaza, the first Intifada broke out in Nablus.

The systematic destruction and marginalization of the middle class resulted in major structural social changes in the old city as many families slid into the lower middle class or even into poverty.

Standards of living

This shift left the per-capita income of 70% of families in the deprived areas of Nablus with less than US$ 3 per day; on average, each of these families consists of eight members. These families spend about 79% of their income on food and housing, and consider health and education to be secondary needs. In these communities, 30% of the population are below 15 years of age.

Palestinian society suffers from high unemployment and poverty; poor neighborhoods are most affected by this. According to official statistics, the poverty rate in the old city of Nablus and its surrounding neighborhood is 50%, and unemployment is at 30%. Unemployment among females is higher than among males. According to the Palestinian Central Bureau of Statistics, general unemployment among males reached 31% in 2013, while female unemployment rates rose to 82.9%. 50.6% of Palestinian graduates aged 20-29 with a BA or intermediate diploma were unemployed in 2012 - a rise from 46.5% in 2011. The unemployment rate in this group was 40.9% in the West Bank and 63.2% in the Gaza Strip. In the old neighborhood of Nablus, the unemployment rate of females in this group is 69%.

A report issued by the United Nations in September 2013 notes that the quality of life is getting worse for Palestinians.

- The population living in slums is increasing - it is high time to take unconventional measures to fight these problems.
- The rate of women's participation in the workforce is below 15%, compared to 67% for men.
- Studies show that there is a clear relationship between poverty and the low level of

education on the one hand, and a rising crime rate among teenagers, school drop-outs, early marriage of girls, and child labor on the other. The percentage of girls who get married at an early age (less than 18 years) is 24%, and the percentage children between the ages of five and 14 who work is 18%.

Studies also indicate that there is a relation between teaching, learning, and improving people's economic situations.

Housing conditions

Of the 4,032 buildings in the old city of Nablus, 33% are damaged; 27% were damaged during the 2002 Israeli invasion and 6% during subsequent invasions. 78% of the residential houses have only two rooms and are occupied by an average of 6 – 10 people. 17% of the houses have poor sanitation services, and 38% poor waste services. Most houses suffer from various problems of habitability, including ventilation, lighting, water leakage, overcrowding, and dampness - some can in fact be considered unsuitable for residential use. About 43% of houses do not receive enough sunshine because buildings are constructed adjacent to each other. 45% of houses are considered overcrowded, and most suffer from noise pollution and humidity.

All these elements leave the people of the old city suffering from anemia, and various skin, respiratory, and other chronic diseases. This situation requires nearby emergency health care centers for the delivery of medical services to residents.

Due to severe space limitations recreational services are almost entirely absent from the old city. This situation is aggravated by the close proximity of homes, the narrowness of passageways, and the increase in the number of children. The only places for children to play and exercise are open spaces in the streets after the end of commercial activities in the evening hours. The old city also lacks nurseries and kindergartens.

In spite of the existence of some institutions and of a variety of activities and programs to improve these conditions, the overall results have weaknesses in efficiency and impact. Why?

- The number of beneficiaries of activities and programs are low.
- The multiplicity of programs.
- Reliance on external funding (projects are implemented when there is funding, but not maintained when funding disappears).
- Insufficient social and economic returns for the population from some projects; no daily follow up or continuity of projects.
- NGOs working in the city of Nablus have no interest in expanding their activities to the old city.
- Lack of integration of the local community into activities and in the identification of priorities and needs.
- Political intervention.

- Strong political affiliation of centers and institutions - professionalism and integrity comes second.

- Lack of centers that provide handicraft and professional training, and that accommodate people with special needs.

Note on Zakat: *The amount of Zakat to be paid by an individual depends on the amount of wealth and the type of assets the individual possesses. The amount of zakat paid on capital assets (e.g. money) is 2.5% Zakat is additionally payable on agricultural goods, precious metals, minerals, and livestock at a rate varying between 2.5 and 20 percent, depending on the type of goods.*

Zakat is only payable on assets continuously owned over one year that are in excess of the nisab, a minimum monetary value. The nisab is calculated after adding the cash value of zakatable assets (gold, silver, cash, stocks, merchandise for business, livestock, etc.). Personal assets such as clothing, household furniture, and one residence are not considered zakatable assets.

Today, in most Muslim countries, zakat is collected through a decentralized and voluntary system where eligible Muslims are expected to pay the zakat based on worship and love of God. Under this voluntary system, Zakat Committees are established, which are tasked with the collection and distribution of zakat funds. According to the Quran, there are eight categories of people who qualify to receive zakat funds:

1. *Those living in absolute poverty*
2. *Those restrained because they cannot meet their basic needs*
3. *The zakat collectors themselves*
4. *Non-Muslims who are sympathetic to Islam or wish to convert to Islam*
5. *People whom one is attempting to free from slavery or bondage. Also includes paying ransom or blood money (Diyya).*
6. *Those who have incurred overwhelming debts while attempting to satisfy their basic needs.*
7. *Those working in God's way.*
8. *Children of the street / Travellers (Ibnus-Sabīl)*

For instance the Zakat Committee of Nablus, which was founded in 1977 by independent good people has two main objectives:
1) Help all poor people;
2) Establish sustainable development.

The committee helps over 3000 poor families by providing financial assistance, food supplies, health services; it also contributes in the payment of tuition and school fees, creating jobs for many young poor youths through establishing many projects like dairy industry.

THE NEED TO RESHAPE AND REBUILD PALESTINIAN CIVIL SOCIETY

Nadia Abu Zaher

Palestinian Legislative Council

1. CHANGES IN THE ROLE OF PALESTINIAN CIVIL SOCIETY

The academic debate does not deal with the changes experienced by civil society after the events of 2006 (see Section 2 below), or with how these events influenced its development or its role in achieving democracy. Civil society is "a school for democracy" and plays an important role in building social capital. The core of the concept of social capital are the links, or relationships formed by interpersonal interactions, regardless of whether public or private, which create trust and cooperation among people. These links will shape behavior and attitudes that will have impacts on society, and create negative or positive social capital.

Civil society can play a role in building positive social capital when it contributes to building trust, reciprocity, and cooperation, which then result in the interaction of people and creates relationships. But it is essential that the goal of this interaction is the general interest of the community and not of private individuals.

In the period under consideration, there were positive and negative impacts on civil society, and to help in the restructuring of civil society, it is necessary to review the positive and negative changes that occurred.

1.1. HOW THE INTIFADA CHANGED THE ROLE OF CIVIL SOCIETY

The first intifada was a crucial phase in the evolution of Palestinian civil society, because of the lack of a Palestinian state and the subordination of Palestinian society to the Israeli occupation. This affected civil society during the uprising, and forced it to play a different role than in most other countries. Palestinian civil society had to fill the place of the absent state, e.g. by providing health and education services, among others.

"People's Committees" were most prominent, the most widespread, and most widely accepted component of Civil Society. During the first intifada, civil society, through the People's Committees, played an important role in promoting public confidence, cooperation, reciprocity, a spirit of volunteerism, and of working for the common instead of the private good. As a result, civil society was able to build positive social capital in Palestinian society.

These People's Committees, which later were dismantled, are an example of the positive role that civil society played during the first intifada. Due to the Israeli occupation, Palestinian citizens needed relief assistance and food, and the Committees worked to provide aid to everyone without distinction. They were prominent examples of the solidarity of the Palestinian people and their integration; their work was mostly based on volunteering and working for the common good rather than for the benefit of a party. They also kept people from being drawn into partisan conflicts, and provided support for the Palestinian community in an emergency.

Moreover, during the uprising, civil society also contributed to the strengthening of democracy; Palestinian civil society is considered to be more democratic than that of other Arab countries. Organizations that were formed during the uprising were characterized by an absence of a centralized leadership, and by non-hierarchical relationships. The People's Committees, for example, were composed of people from all segments of society. They were democratic bodies open to the widest popular participation. Moreover, civil society also played a political role in the struggle against the Israeli occupation.

Reducing the poverty caused by the occupation was a further goal of civil society organizations; the Zakat Committees, in particular, collected donations from rich people and gave them to the poor. Their positive role within the community helped Palestinians gain confidence in and respect for these committees. As a result, civil society depended on the local community and instead of foreigners for its funding. This quick review of the changes in civil society that occurred during the first intifada in 1987 can be summed up as follows:

- the major portion of Palestinian civil society was made up of People's Committees, Zakat Committees, charities, cooperatives, and other associations established by local communities.

- civil society organizations like the Popular and Zakat Committees, and collaborative charities received funding from local sources instead of foreign ones.

- the role of Palestinian civil society differed from those in neighboring countries, because it had to fill the role of the absent Palestinian state by providing health and education services, among others. Another facet of this role was political action and confronting the occupation.

- civil society contributed to promoting positive values in Palestinian society, such as reciprocity, cooperation, trust, and working for the common rather than the good of individuals, political parties, or other associations. It also encouraged a willingness to volunteer for the common good, and thus contributed to the construction of positive social capital.

- Palestinian civil society contributed more significantly to promoting democratic values than the civil societies of neighboring countries. In the occupied territories, civil organizations are characterized by decentralization and horizontal relationships, and participation and membership are open to all.

Manufactory (Olive Oil) – Nablus 1935

1.2. THE IMPACT OF THE PALESTINIAN AUTHORITY ON CIVIL SOCIETY

The creation of the Palestinian Authority (PA) after the Oslo Accords, was another important stage in the evolution of Palestinian civil society. The creation of the Authority contributed to the rapid spread of nongovernmental organizations (NGOs), particularly of those funded from abroad. These NGOs replaced the Popular Committees as the primary constituents of civil society. This diminished the roles played by civil society during the uprising, but new roles emerged in light of the new circumstances.

The new roles included monitoring the performance of the PA, monitoring violations of human rights, and spreading the principles of democracy by focusing on courses, conferences and publications. There were hopes of achieving a democratic transformation through monitoring the executive authority in the areas of human rights, and providing the Legislative Council with the information that is required to fulfill its oversight role.

Civil society was also active in the fight against corruption, which spread after Oslo, and in reforming the PA. Some studies have dismissed the view that civil society contributed significantly to these efforts. Many people who expected civil society to achieve the desired democratic transformation were disappointed.

In their view, the Oslo agreements had a negative impact on the development of civil society and the democratic transformation.

Some studies also indicate that civil society organizations are working according to the agendas of the political parties that created them. These studies suggest that there is great weakness with respect to cooperation and networking among organizations that are active in the same sector or specialization.

Although there were some successes, the new civil society has failed in many ways. Their work is too limited and lacks continuity. In some cases it became more closely allied to the PA than to the people because many of the organizations' leaders were close to the Authority, or were themselves part of the legislature, executive, or judicial authorities. Many of the positive values that civil society exemplified during the uprising declined after Oslo. For example, values such as solidarity, cooperation, and willingness to volunteer for the sake the public good have declined; self-interest became more important than the interest of the community.

As a result of Oslo, the attention that NGOs paid to the common good declined and shifted to personal objectives, and some organizations began to compete over sources of funding.

2. THE NEED TO RESHAPE PALESTINIAN CIVIL SOCIETY

The role of civil society changes from one stage to another, and although these changes were positive during the uprising - building positive social capital, disseminating positive values in Palestinian society, and promoting values of democracy - this was no longer the case in the subsequent stages, particularly after the split between Fatah and Hamas following the 2006 election, which brought the role of civil society to its lowest point. Therefore, there is a need to think carefully about the rebuilding and re-structuring of civil society, and to take note of the positive changes that occurred during the uprising. There is a need for a call to make many changes, but because it will be difficult to address all of them, we will focus only on the most prominent ones.

2.1. THE RESTRUCTURING OF CIVIL SOCIETY

In Palestine, the constituent parts of civil society need to be rebuilt or reshaped, and we can benefit from examining the experience of civil society during the uprising. By looking at this evolution, it becomes evident that the components of cicil society changed. During the uprising family ties and civil society organiza-tions such as People's Committees, cooperative charitable societies, and Zakat Committees were the primary components of civil society. All of these played a positive role in promoting positive values and democracy, and in building positive social capital that strengthened the cohesion of Palestinian society.

There are many reasons why civil society was able to play a positive role during the uprising, but one of these, perhaps the most important, was that cvil society organizations were estab-lished by local communities, and that this made the needs of local society a priority. Popular Committees, for example, were one of the most important parts of civil society. These commit-tees were called "popular" because their work was derived from popular actions and local people. They began with people helping each other. A spirit of solidarity prevailed among them; they wanted to serve each other without expecting compensation.

Consequently, there is another reason that helped popular committees to succeed: they were not working for their own benefit, or for that of individuals, political parties, or third parties – instead they worked for the common good of Palestinian society without charge. Their priority was the public interest.

Zakat Committees were another example of the positive role that civil society organizations played. Their aim was to help Palestinians, particularly those in need. They helped in adopting orphans, supported students in need, provided medical support, and offered financial aid to needy families through monthly payments. Moreover, they contribute to social solidarity among the members of the Palestinian community. Islamic social welfare organizations (including the Zakat Committees) are the largest donors of food in the occupied Palestinian territories after the United Nations Relief and Works Agency (UNRWA).

After Oslo, however, most of the Zakat Committees vanished along with the Popular Committees, and were replaced by non-governmental organizations that were working in accordance with the agendas of external donors. Although we cannot deny the role played by these organizations in terms of publications that promote the spread of democracy, and holding numerous conferences, and seminars, nor their role in monitoring human rights violations by the PA, etc. But in the end, they failed to achieve a democratic transformation, or the reform of the Palesinian Authority.

There are many reasons for the failure of NGOs to achieve a democratic transition in Palestine, but one reason was their shift to working according to outsider donor agendas, which did not prioritize the needs of local communities. For example, NGOs began to prioritize what was called "the fight against the security chaos and misuse of weapons," which spread after the Al-Aqsa Intifada in 2000. That agenda did not reflect internal conditions of the Palestinian community, and the need for weapons to resist the occupation. This agenda also called for "stopping the manifestations of militarism and having a weapon without justification," which reflected the ideas of Western donors who prior-itized the role of security in the fight against terrorism. This approach was rejected by local communities, which distinguished between terrorism and resistance (i.e. the right to resist occupation).

On the other hand, after the 2006 split, organizations established by political parties changed the composition of civil society. These organizations contributed to the deepening of division rather than to reconciliation because their agendas prioritized the interests of the parties that created them, instead of taking into account the public interest of Palestinian society in unity and the bridging the divisions.

This shows that civil society organizations can also play a negative role, which may adversely affect the peace and reconciliation processes between conflicting parties. Some civil society institutions might become divided internally, causing them to lean toward one party or the other. In the case of the organizations estab-lished by Hamas and Fatah, the NGOs adopted the biases of the conflicting parties and served partisan goals, which increased hatred and re-inforced divisions. Even when these organiza-tions took initiatives to improve the situation, they were biased toward one of the conflicting parties, and did not take into account initiatives presented by independent organizations.

In summary, it should be noted that as long as the the organizations of civil society represented the local community, they gave priority to the public interest, understood the needs of the community, and thus made positive contributions. But when these organizations were working in line with foreign agendas, they did not regard the needs of the local community and the common good as a priority and thus failed to achieve the democratic transformation or succeed in building positive social capital.

2.2. REBUILDING THE FUNDING CAPACITY OF CIVIL SOCIETY ORGANIZATIONS

When thinking about the restructuring of Palestinian civil society, funding is one of the issues that needs attention. There is an urgent need to rebuild the financial capacity of civil society organizations to maintain their independence and integrity, to avoid total dependence on funders, regardless of whether they are internal or external parties. Because donors can influence the priorities of civil society organization's, rebuilding the financial capacity of civil society organizations will increase their acceptance by the Palestinian community. This is especially important now that this community has lost much confidence in civil society institutions. Therefore, it is necessary to know from where organizations derive funding for their activities and what the purpose of this funding is.

In this regard the experience of civil society organizations during the uprising can again be useful. The Popular Committees relied on self-funding, i.e. funding from voluntary contributions of local people, including many contributions from wealthy donors. Although some funding and donations did come from Arab countries and their citizens, such funding was not attached to specific conditions.

Zakat Committees (Islamic charity) are another good example of civil society organizations that adopted self-financing approaches. They have a great deal of legitimacy among all Palestinians - even among secular leftists. According to Nathan Brown, the local communities respect the Zakat Committees' authenticity and ability to achieve funding without dependence on Western donors. They also gained the trust of Palestinian society in general; a survey has shown that Palestinian society has high trust in Zakat Committees – achieving an approval rate of 58%. - compared to other civil society organizations, and to institutions of the PA.

Zakat Committees do not depended exclusively on the funding received from the local community, they have also developed other funding sources, which prevent them from falling prey to foreign agendas. Some of the committees developed their local community by implementing projects to increase their self-financing capacities and to engage in sustainable development. The Nablus Zakat Committees are a good example; they developed: a project for orphans, a specialized hospital for eye treatments, an all-day clinic, and a yogurt factory. In addition a large portion of their local funding is collected from Zakat payments and the proceeds of real estate.

However, after Oslo, a problem arose concerning the funding of civil society, particularly of NGOs. There was a shift to dependence on foreign funding and thus a requirement to cater to the agendas of foreign donors. To receive funds, a civil society organization must comply with the terms of the donors, which then affects the trust of the local community.

Harvest Time – Nablus 1930

A distinction is normally made between recipient organizations and donor institutions - each has different policies, goals and agendas, but those of the donor tend to be imposed on the recipient. Donors appear eager to provide aid, and grants to achieve "development", "democracy" or "human rights", etc. But all too often this is a cover under which donor organizations hide their real agendas. They use some of the recipient NGOs" to achieve goals on the donor's behalf.

Moreover, the civil society organizations' dependence on external financing affects their ability to continue – in fact, they are unable to continue their normal activities without external donations. An interruption to the grants can lead to the closure of these organizations, or in the best case, force them to reduce their activities, and this is indeed what happened to many Palestinian NGOs.

There are also risks connected with local funding, especially when it comes from political parties, because it might be politically oriented, and worsen existing divisions. For example, after Hamas won the elections to the Palestinian Legislative Council in 2006, and Fatah believed that civil associations affiliated to Hamas had a role in this victory, Fatah created pro-Fatah non-governmental organizations. As a result, donors rushed to fund these new NGOs, which sought to empower Fatah over Hamas in Gaza.

2.3. REORIENTING CIVIL SOCIETY TOWARDS VOLUNTEERISM

It is widely believed that the most important mechanism for the generation of social capital is social interaction, membership in voluntary associations, civic participation, and that these generate democratic values. Accordingly, in reshaping civil society the principle of volunteering for the community must be reemphasized. Popular participation and volunteering will contribute to the promotion of positive social capital and to the spread of democracy.

Here too, we can benefit from the experience of civil society during the uprising, when it operated on the basis of volunteerism. For example, Zakat Committees included members from different backgrounds on a volunteer basis – these members were not allowed to take money for their service. Widespread willingness to participate in volunteer activities was also encouraged by the People's Committees, which led to the spreading of mutuality in Palestinian communities. People offered their services to others voluntarily and cooperatively without expecting anything in return. They believed that others would do the same for them, and that the People's Committees were working for the common good without looking for the material return or serving partisan or private objectives.

Participants in voluntary work came from all segments of society, and not a specific class, group, or party. Studies have indicated that the involvement of the majority of civil society organizations in the Palestinian national struggle earned the respect of the popular masses. It was observed that the willingness to participate in voluntary work declined after Oslo and the 2006 split. A study has shown that the total number of volunteers in the NGO sector declined from 64,936 volunteers in the year 2000 to 53,622 volunteers in 2006. The vast majority of those working currently in civil society organizations in Palestine are paid, even the so-called volunteers; they volunteer in order to gain experience that qualifies them to enter the labor market. Many civil society organizations consider the members of registered public assemblies to be permanent volunteers though the facts suggest the contrary. In 2007, after the split, the increased number of NGOs did not result in an increase in the number of volunteers - on the contrary, the number of volunteers actually declined.

THE "OSLO SYSTEM" AND THE WAR ON GAZA

Helga Baumgarten
Bir Zeit University

From early July to late August 2014, Israel's war on Gaza raged: For 50 days, from July 7 to the ceasefire on the evening of August 26, the Israeli army bombed and shelled the Gaza Strip in the longest war ever fought by Israel. During this time, the Palestinian armed organizations, led by Hamas and Islamic Jihad, fired what were usually homemade rockets at Israel, reaching as far as Tel Aviv, Jerusalem, and even Eilat. The victims in Gaza were mainly civilians - between 70% and 80% of the more than 2,100 killed. On the Israeli side, 66 soldiers were killed in direct clashes with Palestinian militants, while Palestinian rockets killed six civilians. The asymmetry of this war is re-flected in the numbers and needs no further explanation.

September 2014 marked the 21st year of the signing of the Oslo Accords. On September 13, 1993, Israel and the PLO agreed to end the decades-long Israeli–Palestinian conflict and pledged to reach a solution within 5 years. All pending problems were to be resolved through negotiation.

Such a solution has not been reached, and its chances of success now seem more unlikely than ever. Several Israeli Army (IDF) attacks on Palestinian territories and the three wars waged against the people of the Gaza Strip within 7 years (2008/9, 2012, and 2014) make such an outlook seem even less realistic.

This paper analyses the relation between the "Oslo system" and the Gaza war of 2014.

THE "OSLO SYSTEM"

There is not just one Oslo, but rather three Oslos.

Oslo I stands for the hope and the desire for peace. Oslo I always remained wishful thinking, although it is set at the center of the Palestinian political and public discourse, the discourse of the international community, and that of political representatives worldwide. But Oslo I has never been implemented, not even in a rudimentary way.

The term Oslo II refers to the agreements between the declaration of principles on September 13, 1993 and the signature of the Sharm el-Sheikh Memorandum on September 4, 1999. There is no space to get into the details here, but from a Palestinian perspective, they were disastrous: Oslo II did not contain the notion of a Palestinian state, did not define a strategy for the actual implementation of the agreements (i.e. an acceptable negotiation mechanism), and, above all, it did not create a mutually acceptable set of advantages to be gained through compliance with the agreements, let alone a timeframe in which those measures could be implemented.[1]

Oslo III, the "Oslo System" as I shall call it, will be examined in more detail. This analysis will show how the recent war on Gaza is related to this system and why it is the only way to explain the war as such. So, what exactly is the "Oslo System?" In the following, I shall analyze six of the key pillars of Oslo III.

1. The occupation of Palestinian land is maintained, and the colonial settlements remain in place and expand continuously; new settlements are built under the cover of the expansion of older ones. The underlying principle is simple: Only the occupation allows Israel to build and expand the settlements, and this, in turn, necessitates the perpetuation of the occupation.

2. The Oslo System forces the PA (Palestinian Authority, known as the "Sulta") to pointless and countless new rounds of, obviously unfruitful negotiations with the Israeli government.

3. The Oslo System forces the PA to participate in a so-called "Security Cooperation." Put simply, his means that the PA actively polices the Occupied Territories for the occupier, as stated in the Declaration of Principles of September 1993 and expounded in more detail in the 1995 Interim Agreement. Thus, the occupied, the Palestinians, help their occupiers, the Israelis, to maintain and perpetuate their occupation. This situation is unique in the history of national liberation movements, as Edward Said critically assessed as early as 1993.[2]

4. Meanwhile, the process of fragmentation imposed on Palestine and its society is driven to new heights.[3] Along with the geographic and social fragmentation, the Oslo System added the fragmentation of the political landscape of Palestine, which was successfully prevented after the first summit conference of Camp David in 1978. This fragmentation emerged with the beginning of the Oslo agreements in 1993. It was implemented systematically in the following years and is maintained until today.

5. The implementation of the Paris Agreements and the associated integration of the Palestinian economy into the neo-liberal international monetary system, and its extreme dependence on the Israeli economy created a permanent economic crisis. These mechanisms benefit an almost obscenely rich economic elite while the majority of the population has become impoverished and is increasingly dependent on bank loans. Thus, the gap between the rich and the poor is growing constantly.[4]

6. The progressive international integration through the recognition of Palestinian statehood

marginalized Palestine in the region. The Palestine conflict, which continues to be the central problem in the region, is overshadowed by other conflicts such as the Arab uprisings since 2011, the "Iran problem," the new "Cold War," and the expansion of Islamic State ISIS.

COLONIAL SETTLEMENTS REQUIRE THE OCCUPATION AND THE OCCUPATION REQUIRES COLONIAL SETTLEMENTS TO MAINTAIN LEGITIMACY

The Oslo system allows Israel to strengthen its control over the entire West Bank both figuratively and physically. The life of every Palestinian is controlled by the occupation, including the:

- Freedom of movement within and out of the occupied territories;

- Problem of papers/documents: The "registration office" is in Israeli hands; thus an Israeli institution decides who is granted residence and who is not;

- Legal system: Israeli military courts try Palestinians who are accused of "security breaches";

- Building permits and house demolitions;

- Control over water consumption: Referring to the current debate on this topic, the President of the European Parliament, Martin Schulz, held a speech in the Knesset in February 2014 in which he drew on accurate numbers to heavily criticize Israeli policies. This led to a predictably harsh reaction from Knesset MPs. When we examine the total consumption in agriculture, industry, and drinking water, an Israeli citizen uses almost five times as much water as a Palestinian: precisely 646 liters per day compared to 133 liters. If we only consider the water used in agriculture, the Israeli consumption (368 liters) is six-and-a-half times higher than that of Palestinians (57 liters). Daily, an Israeli consumes 278 liters of drinking and industrial process water, while a Palestinian has only 77 liters, which is 3.6 times less. The World Health Organization considers 100 liters of drinking water per day as the minimum for a decent life.[5]

This system of occupation is maintained by Israel with all its military might. Again, I want to present a few numbers to illustrate this. In the year 1993, at the beginning of the Oslo negotiation process, the Israeli state allowed 112,000 people to settle in the West Bank and another 153,000 in East Jerusalem, which is a total of 265,000 settlers that year alone.

In the year 2000, the year that Oslo II should have produced a solution to the conflict, the number of settlers had almost doubled, reaching 193,000 in the West Bank and 172,000 in East Jerusalem, which brings the total to 365,000 settlers.

The year 2010/11 saw a further massive increase in settlers. Their number in the West Bank increased to 328,000 and in East Jerusalem to 200,000 - a total of 528,000. Today, the estimated number of settlers is 350,000 in the West Bank and slightly more than 200,000 in East Jerusalem. This amounts to 550,000 settlers. To contrast these figures, there are about 2.5 million Palestinians living in the West Bank and an additional 300,000 in East Jerusalem. (Until 2005, about 7,500 settlers lived in Gaza; today, 1.7 to 1.8 million Palestinians live there.)[6]

Even this quick look at the demographic data shows that Israel is systematically undermining Oslo I, the Oslo of peace and hope, and turning its initial purpose upside down. Instead of using the Oslo System to achieve the Two-State Solution, it is using ther System to make it impossible. On the economic level, the same pattern is repeated. Instead of handing over occupied land to the Palestinians, settlements expand. To put this into numbers: 20 years after Oslo, 61% of Palestinian land is economically inaccessible, creating an annual loss of $3.5 billion (according to a World Bank report of October 2013) - a figure that represents 35% of Palestinian GDP.[7]

Without the complicity of United States, the EU (which has not strictly enforced the guidelines adopted in July 2013), and other international actors this expansion of the Oslo System would never have been possible.

SECURITY COOPERATION AND POLITICAL FRAGMENTATION

The Oslo System forces the PA to maintain security cooperation with Israel. In effect, they engage in policing their population for the occupation. Thus, the aim of this cooperation, and the main objective of the security services of the PA, is to control any opposition to the occupation. This inevitably leads to a permanent conflict with other major political actors such as the largest political movement, the Hamas.

This conflict is therefore of a systematic nature and inherent to the Oslo System. A short look at inter-Palestinian relations illustrates this. In 2003, at the end of the 2nd Intifada, all Palestinian organizations, led by Fatah and Hamas, decided to embrace the notion of the primacy of politics over violence. This led to a period of elections in the Occupied Territories: the local elections in 2004–2005, the presidential elections of January 2005, and the parliamentary elections of January 2006.

Immediately after the parliamentary elections, the inherently conflict-oriented Oslo System began to come into effect. Hamas won the elections with a program aiming to achieve Palestinian statehood within the borders of 1967 with East Jerusalem as its capital and the recognition of Israel. Fatah refused to submit to the government of national unity offered by Hamas. Instead, Fatah began, under the leadership of Mohammed Dahlan, to mobilize the secret service and armed factions. This mobilization led to a coup against the elected Hamas party with the full support and even initiative of the United States.[8] As Alvaro de Soto, the UN special envoy for the Middle East Peace Process in Palestine, wrote quite bluntly in his final report: "Before going on, I want to stress that, in effect, a National Unity Government with a compromise platform along the lines of Mecca might have been achieved soon after the election, in February or March 2006, had the US not led the Quartet [author's note: US, EU, UN, Russia] to set impossible demands, and opposed a NUG in principle."[9]

Under these circumstances, and considering the interior tensions between the political camps, bloody fights erupted leading to the split between the Fatah-controlled West Bank and the Hamas-controlled Gaza Strip. This territorial fragmentation further deepened the initial split that evolved after the founding of the State of Israel. In the meantime, the Palestinian actors themselves stabilized and extended this fragmentation by focusing on their own group's immediate interests. Though there have been Palestinian politicians who, with massive popular support, tried to enact a political U-turn, all successive Israeli governments were concerned with stifling any attempts at reconciliation. Israel simply does not allow the Palestinians to overcome their detrimental division. The aim of their policies was, and still is, to ensure the continuation of the occupation and thus to expand their colonial settlements, that is, to prevent a Palestinian state. Those policies have been conducted with the full support of the United States and with hardly any criticism from the European Union. Soon after, a transparent pattern evolved: Whenever the Palestinian parties had agreed on a unification process, massive pressure was exerted on Fatah to decide between "terror", i.e. reconciliation with Hamas, or upholding the terms of the so-called "Peace Process" with Israel. This was accompanied by pressure from Washington to agree to a new round of negotiations initiated by the United States. These negotiations failed, as did all previous peace attempts, because the Israeli side was unwilling to take a first step toward the implementation of a Two-State Solution.

THE GOVERNMENT OF NATIONAL UNITY 2014: CAN THE PALESTINIANS CAST OFF THE SHACKLES OF THE "OSLO SYSTEM?"

The failure of the Kerry Initiative after months of fruitless negotiations from the summer of 2013 to the spring of 2014 led to a completely new constellation. The Palestinians, led by Fatah under Mahmoud Abbas and Hamas under Ismail Haniyeh, agreed on a national unity government that was sworn into office and began its work in May 2014. For the first time since the beginning of the Oslo peace process, the United States were prepared to tolerate such a government - a government consisting of technocrats without the official involvement of Fatah or Hamas. The EU was prepared to go a step further and launched direct cooperation with the new government.

In this new constellation, the United States acknowledged for the first time that the refusal of the Israeli government to stop their settlement program was the main obstacle to resolving the conflict. Considering this, even a politician as obsessively focused on negotiations as Palestinian President Mahmoud Abbas had to embark on a new course of action. Under his leadership, the PA agreed to form the first Government of National Unity, which is still in power today. At the same time, he applied for, and in many cases achieved, admission to several UN organizations.

Bethlehem - 1930

How is one to judge this new approach by Palestinian politicians? Are the Palestinians, especially the PA in Ramallah under Mahmoud Abbas, ready to cast off the shackles of the "Oslo System"?

The crucial first question concerns the motives of both parties to agree to submit to such a government of national unity.

The answer is obvious when one considers Mahmoud Abbas' decision. The failure of the Kerry initiative, the relentless expansion of the colonial settlement project, and the ongoing violence of the Israeli occupation left no space for alternatives to Abbas. Judging this policy shift remains a hard task. Will Ramallah continue to walk this path, or is Abbas simply waiting, as he has done so often before, for a signal from Tel Aviv to once again engage in doomed negotiations?

Two decisions of Ramallah clarify how unstable the new political course actually is. Although Abbas signed a number of membership applications to international organizations, the crucial signature, which truly points in new directions, is still missing: the ratification of the Rome Statute and therefore membership of the International Criminal Court in The Hague. Despite massive pressure from Palestinian civil society as well as from all Palestinian parties[10], Abbas is still unwilling to ratify the Statute to this very day. Contrary to public statements by Foreign Minister Riad al-Malki (who supported signing the Rome Statute in order to take Israel

before the International Criminal Court in The Hague), a letter from the Prosecutor of the Tribunal shows that the PA was not prepared to declare a lawsuit initiated from Gaza to be an official Palestinian action and to thus set the legal process in motion. The elites surrounding Abbas want to avoid the International Criminal Court, as internal information from a PLO Executive Committee meeting indicates. (Editor's Note: The Palestinian Authority formally joined the International Criminal Court in April of 2015.)

An even more problematic issue at hand is Abbas' support for the main achievement of the Israelis within the framework of the Oslo System: the security cooperation. In a speech addressed to the Israeli Peace Forces in Ramallah, he called the security cooperation "holy".[11]

Now Hamas' motives for approving of the Government of National Unity and cooperation with the PA must be examined.

The decisive change in the region seems to have been the end of the Muslim Brotherhood led government in Egypt due to a military coup. For the first time since the electoral victory of Hamas in 2006 and its exclusive control over the Gaza Strip since June 2007 its borders were sealed, not only to the east and the north by Israel's blockade, but also to its southern neighbor, Egypt. Thus, the entire Gaza Strip is not only sealed off by Israel but, more importantly, by Egypt as well, closing off the vital supply line through the Rafah tunnels. The land, society, and each and every individual are now facing an economic disaster simultaneously with a veritable political crisis within the Brotherhood-based Hamas.

Faced with a virtually total blockade, approaching Fatah offered Hamas a way out. The Government of National Unity was the first step. It remains impossible to determine whether Hamas saw this newly arising situation as an opportunity to break free from the Oslo System altogether.

The failure of the Kerry initiative, the widespread frustration among the population regarding "peace negotiations", plus the new course of action by Abbas might have led to such a scenario. It is equally unclear whether a promising new strategy of resistance was being discussed or intended for a future confrontation that would have offered an alternative to the Oslo System.

This leads to an important question: Has there been, from the start, a politically calculated scenario involving a direct military confrontation with the occupation forces and thus undoubtedly an intention to break free from the shackles of Oslo? The massive expansion of the militarily usable tunnel system under the Gaza Strip and its eastern and northern borders does point toward this possibility. Parallel to this development, Hamas' military preparations suggest that a new conflict is looming on the horizon. Is Hamas expecting a new war and preparing for that? Was the entry into the Government of National Unity an attempt to get Fatah and the PA on its side, or did it simply endorse this agreement to obtain more time to prepare for the next war?

Two test cases show the problem of inter-Palestinian cooperation:

- the kidnapping of three young settlers in the West Bank in June 2014, and

- Israel's third war against Hamas controlled Gaza in the summer of 2014 (July–August) named "Operation Protective Edge" in the Israeli attempt to trivialize it.

TEST CASE I: KIDNAPPING AND MURDER OF THREE YOUNG SETTLERS IN THE OCCUPIED SOUTH WEST BANK

The kidnapping of three young settlers near Hebron, an area under full military control, gave the Netanyahu government the long-awaited chance to launch a massive blow against Hamas and to start undermining the Government of National Unity.

Tel Aviv expected that Hamas would break away from the unity government after being attacked, because Ramallah was sticking to the security cooperation. This, however, was a miscalculation. Instead of widening the gap between Fatah and Hamas, popular support for Abbas in the West Bank collapsed. Weakened by the failure of the Kerry Initiative, massively criticized for upholding the security cooperation under such circumstances, and being regarded as a caricature of himself, Abbas fought for his political survival in June. He was obviously not ready to take the first step to free himself from the shackles of the Oslo System. He did not abandon the security cooperation nor did he sign the Rome Statute. Instead, he held on to the boundaries set by the US.

View of Jerusalem (Al Quds) from the Mount Olivet – 1940

TEST CASE II: ISRAEL'S WAR ON GAZA OR "OPERATION PROTECTIVE EDGE"

Israel's war on Hamas was in reality a ruthless war against the entire Palestinian people in Gaza. Could the new united front policy of the Palestinians, especially Abbas' PA in Ramallah, endure? Would it survive the war, the subsequent negotiations, and the period of reconstruction in the Gaza Strip?[12]

Two issues urgently need to be solved:

- Paying the salaries of the newly appointed PA employees who were hired after Abbas, in 2006/7, commanded that all PA employees should refuse to work under the new Hamas government

- Negotiations over lifting the Gaza blockade and whether or not Abbas is serious about ending the security cooperation and addressing the UN over the question of Israeli occupation[13]

Today, only a few weeks after the end of the war, a solution to the conflict seems further away than ever before. Disputes between Hamas and Fatah escalate on a daily basis, further fueled by information spread by Israeli security sources that Hamas was attempting a coup against the PA. It seems as if Abbas more readily believes information from Israeli sources than from his own coalition partner. This also illustrates the desperate attempts by Tel Aviv to further undermine the Government of National Unity.

The focus of Palestinian politics is on the power struggle between Fatah and Hamas - not on the future of the Gaza Strip, nor the future of Palestine, nor on the end of the occupation, nor freedom or political independence.

Desperately attempting to block Hamas' rise in popularity, Fatah members are engaging in unprecedented forms of verbal polemic against their rival. Fatah and PA representatives do not hold Israel accountable for the recent war, but Hamas. Moreover, Abbas accuses Hamas of wanting to destabilize the West Bank in order to attempt a coup against him and his PA. The polemics have gone to such extremes that an official representative of the Government of National Unity portrayed Hamas as being non-Palestinian.[14]

As we see, the Oslo System continues to work efficiently.

THE PALESTINIAN PUBLIC AND THE OSLO SYSTEM

In the meantime, the Palestinian public has adopted a clear position. According to a survey conducted between the end of August and the beginning of September 2014,[15] 53% of the population believe that armed resistance is the most efficient way to achieve Palestinian statehood. Only 22% consider negotiations as being promising and only 20% prefer peaceful mass resistance.

As many as 86% were in favor of rocket attacks on Israel until the end of the blockade, and 79% see Israel as the party responsible for the outbreak of the war. Just as many believe that Hamas won the war.

These numbers show a reversal of the dominant political positions since 2007. For the first time, Ismail Haniyeh, the Prime Minister elected in 2006/7, later deposed by Abbas, would win with 61% to 31%. In parliamentary elections, Hamas would gain 46% of the votes compared to only 31% for Fatah.

In contrast to Fatah and the government in Ramallah, 83% of the population want the salaries of employees in Gaza, who have been hired by the separate Hamas government, to be paid by the Government of National Unity. According to the poll, control of border crossings (51%) and the reconstruction of Gaza (44%) should be central to the policies of a new government. The general optimism of the population regarding reconciliation between Hamas and Fatah has risen sharply to 69%, and 60% support a unity government formed by both parties instead of the current government of technocrats.

WHAT WILL HAPPEN TO THE OSLO SYSTEM AFTER THE WAR ON GAZA?

What is the current policy for future Palestine of its two most important representatives, Fatah and Hamas? What is the position of the Palestinian public? Will Israel maintain the "Oslo System?" Who on the Palestinian side is ready to break out of this system or destroy it?

Mahmoud Abbas and his political elite in Ramallah seem to be trapped in Oslo to such an extent that they cannot take future-oriented steps. On the contrary, they are doing everything in their power to preserve a system from which they have benefited financially ever since 1993/4. Hamas, on the other hand, tried to break the bonds of the system through military resistance. At the same time, it showed a willingness to accept a two-state solution and to act within this framework. The Palestinian public supports Hamas in their course. To this date, however, no real success has been achieved. Palestinian society lacks the will and ability to become involved in a violent mass resistance and rebellion - the only act that could smash the Oslo system. One way to achieve this would be to strengthen the BDS movement. This is now being widely implemented in the Occupied Territories through a boycott of at least some Israeli goods, which have dominated the Palestinian market since 1967.

[1] Rabin's speech, "no data is holy". New York Times, 14 December 1993

[2] Edward Said, The Morning After, London Review of Books 15.20: 21 October 1993

[3] Meron Benvenisti, United We Stand, Haaretz 28 January 2010

[4] Alaa Tartir and Jeremy Wildemann, Can Oslo's failed aid model be laid to rest, Al-Shabaka 19.9.2013 and Tariq Dana, The Palestinian Capitalists have gone too far, Al-Shabaka 14.1.2014

[5] Clemens Messerschmid, Wasser und Krieg, Süddeutsche Zeitung 10.3.2014 and Clemens Messerschmid: 20 Jahre Oslo – Bilanz im Wassersektor, inamo Nr. 76, Winter 2013

[6] Foundation for Middle East Peace: www.fmep.org

[7] Animation by the World Bank on www.maannews.net 11.9.2014

[8] David Rose, The Gaza Bombshell, Vanity Fair April 2008: www.vanityfair.com

[9] De Soto Report 2007 as quoted in: Helga Baumgarten, Kampf um Palästina, Freiburg 2013: p. 157

[10] Polls August 2014: 84% of the population support signing the statute. PSR Special Gaza War Poll: www.pcpsr.org/eng/special-gaza-war-poll

[11] Amira Hass, Haaretz, 8 July 2014

[12] Protocol of the meeting between Abbas and Meshal in Qatar in: Al-Akhbar, 5/6 September 2014: http://english.al-akhbar.com/print21402

[13] see detailed Qatar - Protocol in Al-Akhbar

[14] Al-Akhbar (Qatar – Protocol), Fatah representative Ahmad Assaf in Al-Mayadeen, 30.8.2014 and a speech of a Fatah official hold on the PASSIA seminar on 9.9.2014, Jerusalem at which the author was present

[15] PSR Special Gaza War Poll: www.pcpsr.org/eng/special-gaza-war-poll

BACKGROUND INFORMATION

From the 7th to the 9th of November 2014, our concluding conference for the 2-year EZA-Project, "We are Nablus" (financed by the OFID, the OPEC Fund for International Development) took place in the Afro-Asian Institute under the title "Reclaiming Palestine: Empowering the Marginalized - The Social and Economical Reconstruction of Palestinian Society under Foreign Occupation."

In addition to participants in the project, the speakers were from the partner-NGO, SCCS, Abdull Jabar Khalili of the An-Najah National University (Palestine), Adnan Odeh (SCCS project leader), and Muzan Shoqua from Nablus, as well as political scientist Helga Baumgartner. To house the conference, we asked the Afro-Asian Institute (AAI, Türkenstraße 3, 1090 Vienna) whether facilities could be rented. After in-depth discussions, the management of the AAI proposed to organize the conference as a cooperative venture. In several meetings with our new partner, it seemed important to us to point out the political pressure that is brought to bear whenever events about Palestine in general and events of "Dar al Janub" in particular are organized.

In this dialogue, it was important to us to point out the ever-recurring accusations and allegations that are raised against our organization in the run-up of every conference of "Dar al Janub". Nevertheless, the management of AAI maintained its proposal to organize the conference in cooperation.

A few days before the conference was to begin, representatives of the IKG (the Jewish Religious Community in Austria) contacted the management of the AAI, the archdiocese of Vienna, and other associated institutions, and demanded with increasing vehemence that the AAI distance itself from the cooperative arrangement. The revealing E-mail correspondence that took place over a span of weeks is in our possession. However, in view of the unclear legal situation, we will not publish this correspondence here without the agreement of the involved parties (AAI, IKG, and archdiocese).

In a final E-mail message, a representative of the IKG unmistakably demanded of the AAI management that distancing itself from the event was necessary for the continuation of inter-religious cooperation: "Either dialogue with the Jewish community, or the 'Reclaiming Palestine' event". In the end, a letter appeared in the IKG-magazine "The Community Insider" of December 2014 in which the Director of the AAI distanced the Institute retroactively from the conference.

Tiberias and the Lake of Gennesaret – 1936

LETTER OF THE IKG TO THE DIRECTOR OF THE AFRO-ASIAN INSTITUTE, NOVEMBER 11, 2014

Dear Father Matyssek,

with regret, I have learned of an event entitled "Reclaiming Palestine" that took place from July 9 to 14 of 2014 in the facilities of the Afro-Asian Institute, and of the subsequent correspondence with a member of our Board of Management, Mr. Schnarch – particularly, because the Catholic Church bears a special responsibility for this Institute.

"Dar Al Janub" is the successor organization of the Sedunia society (the composition of which can be characterized in essence as a mixture of radical leftists and converts to Islam), which, years ago, attacked a memorial service for the Kristallnacht pogrom in front of the former synagogue in the Zirkusgasse, and attempted to disperse it using a "Rollkommando" (ed.: originally a motorized armed Nazi unit used to terrorize and murder civilians; also "hired thugs"). After even otherwise extremely anti-Israel circles rejected this action, the society was reorganized under the name "Dar al Janub".

The "Remapping Palestine" event was scheduled for the same date as the night of the pogrom as a provocative gesture. I assume that this coincidence of timing was not apparent to you. Anti-Semites, regardless of whether left, or right in orientation, are not partners for dialogue with us. In truth, "Dar Al Janub" is not interested in dialogue, and is not able to approach its "opponents" with even a minimal measure of acceptance. The "Alibi-Jews" that they invited as conversation partners are persons from the extreme-left milieu, who are in no way representative of Israeli society, just as a radical-right "Burschenschafter" (ed.: member of a German student fraternity) could not speak meaningfully about the Austrian nation.

The title "Reclaiming Palestine" obscures a rejection of the Oslo Accords, the demand for the liquidation of the Jewish State, and the call for boycott activities such as "Don't buy from Israeli firms". All matters that a close examination of the Facebook Page www.facebook.com/events/494067560728888, or on the website www.dar-al-janub.net/nablus.htm could not have escaped your attention.

In any case, the peaceful and constructive words of Pope Francis were not implemented by the acceptance of such guests. I must therefore urgently request that in future you exercise more care.

Best regards

Raimund Fastenbauer
General Secretary of the IKG Vienna

REPLY OF THE AFRO-ASIAN INSTITUTE, NOVEMBER 17, 2014

Dear Mr. Fastenbauer,

in the name of the AAI-Vienna I would like to apologize to the Jewish Religious Community (IKG) and its members, among whom the event "Reclaiming Palestine: Empowering the Marginalized – The Social and Economical Reconstruction of Palestinian Society under Foreign Occupation," which took place in our facilities, caused great concern. Given the current state of knowledge, it would not have taken place in our Institute in this form.

There must not be any doubt that the AAI-Vienna will not open the door to extremism, either now or in the future, and that it will not offer any space to anti-Israel or anti-Semitic ideas. This applies to our staff and to our guests.

It is the duty of the AAI-Vienna to advocate the "promotion of peace, understanding among peoples, and justice". It accomplishes this by making space for encounters between individuals, through exchanges among cultures, and dialogue among religions, in which mutual interest and trust grow and bridges can be built. In so doing, we want to take every person und his or her concerns seriously, and to walk with them on a path to a better understanding.

In the case under discussion, these principles were also our guideline in arriving at a decision for a limited cooperation with "Dar al Janub." The purpose was to present a project "The Palestinian Women Economic & Cultural Empowerment's Project in the Governorate of Nablus". It appeared to be a contribution, which, based on its humanitarian character, could initiate a dialogue.

Unfortunately, we neglected to be attentive to the fact that even the title of the event is contrary to our goal and raises justified fears. In addition, the positions for which "Dar al Janub" stands in public, or that they promote, have the potential of creating damage rather than promoting a constructive dialogue. As a result, this allowed the impression to arise in the public and to you that we did not decisively oppose any kind of anti-Semitic tendencies.

Instead of building bridges, we damaged the foundation on which they must stand - your trust. We would be personally touched if this trust would suffer enduring damage, and we speak here also in the name of all our staff, who, for 25 years, has been partly engaged in the Jewish-Christian dialogue.

We always strive to live up to the responsibility for society that we share and to the tasks that Cardinal König set for us at our foundation. Consequently, we will use this occasion to increase our attentiveness so that our competence in cross-cultural and inter-religious dialogue will grow.

Best regards

Christoph Matyssek, Director
Nikolaus Heger, Managing Director

OPEN LETTER FROM DAR AL JANUB TO FATHER CHRISTOPH MATYSSEK, DIRECTOR OF THE AFRO-ASIAN INSTITUTE, VIENNA

...there are numerous people in the world who are in hell because they are too dependent on the judgment of others.

(Jean-Paul Sartre)

It is even possible to change the past. Historians prove it again and again.

(Jean-Paul Sartre)

Dear Father Matyssek,

with astonishment we note your rapid about-face concerning our cooperatively organized event, "Reclaiming Palestine", which took place in November 2014. We were especially dismayed by the defamatory way that you chose, because long before and during our joint event, we had direct and intensive discussions with you and the Afro-Asian Institute (AAI). Now we learn from the Journal of the Jewish religious community that your opinion of our organization and the event on which we had agreed has taken a U-turn. Of course, we are disappointed that you chose to proceed in this manner instead of seeking the way of open, direct debate, especially because, as the Director of the AAI, you champion inter-religious and inter-cultural dialogue.

As you evidently decided to give in to the ultimatum of the IKG, which had threatened to *break off the inter-religious dialogue unless the AAI retroactively distanced itself from this cooperatively organized event, we feel compelled to publish the correspondence between the IKG, the Archdiocese Vienna, the AAI, and ourselves. Moreover, we must contradict two decisive points in your letter to the IKG, which was published in "The Community Insider" December 2014, p. 19.*

We can well understand the political pressure that you and your institute were and are still subjected to. Likewise, we understand that you, as Director of the AAI bear important responsibilities. For this reason, we sought to have a dialogue with you and the management of the AAI starting more than 8 months ago, and initially requested only to rent rooms for the event that was to mark the end of one of our projects. The proposal to organize the event in cooperation came from the AAI, and, naturally, we were very happy about it. Nevertheless, in many conversations, we openly discussed the possible pressures from groups supportive of the Israeli government's policies, and comprehensively presented to you the political orientation of our group, as well as the attempts at defaming our organization. Not least, because of this open conversational climate either you or the AAI decided to not only support the event as a cooperating partner, but to give the opening remarks and to make the acquaintance of the invited guests from Palestine. In the run-up to our cooperation, we openly discussed with you, the allegations, which border on character assassination, that Mr. Fastenbauer and the IKG persistently spread, just as we presented the entire 10-year history of our organization and the controversies that our events occasioned.

Obviously, having identical viewpoints is not a precondition for cooperation. However, we do not view differing position on the part of the AAI and Dar al Janub as something divisive, but rather as an enrichment that cross-fertilizes. In our cooperation, no one would have demanded agreement on views and perspectives without reservations. Working together critically is always a fruitful stimulus to scrutinize our own work, and if necessary to correct it. In your biased letter to Mr. Fastenbauer you change the actual course of the controversy in short order, and alter the history of our cooperation. Your silence about the baseless accusations of Mr. Fastenbauer, and your virtually approving formulations are a sad example of the often fainthearted attitude of the Catholic Church. Time and again, there were and still are representatives of the church, who's courageous attitudes defied pressure and accepted drastic or even life-threatening risks to expose problems and injustices and to give new impulses for change. The South African Archbishop Desmond Tutu and the Irish Priest Hugh O'Flaherty are two shining examples of the courage of Catholic or Anglican dignitaries that remained faithful to their convictions.

Without objection, you let stand the assertion that our event was planned on November 9th as a provocative, distasteful reminiscence of the "Kristallnacht" pogrom, although you know very

well that this date was selected by the AAI from several of our proposed dates as the sole possibility during that time. Nor does your reply contain even one word about Mr. Schnarch's arguments that go off the rails, or his hostile and slanderous E-mails that are full of verbal violence and are directed against you and your institute. Obviously, you also consider it irrelevant in your reply, that Rabbi Schlomo Hofmeister, in an E-mail message to us, not only denies the violence of the occupation and of Jewish settlers against Palestinians, but also the existence of the Palestinian people itself. Nor does it seem to disturb you that Mr. Fastenbauer of the IKG once again defames as "Alibi-Jews" all Jewish dissidents, and all Jews that are critical of the government and state of Israel, and thus claims for himself the right to define who is a "real Jew". This has direct impacts on our friends in Israel, whom Mr. Fastenbauer labels as "Alibi-Jews", because their anti-racist engagement not only draws state repression, but also exposes them to physical threats due to the racist consensus that is shared by large parts of Israeli society.

Although your statement seems at first sight largely passive, conciliatory, and defensive, your subtle argumentation is almost more violent, as the written off-the-rails statements of Mr. Schnarch. You know that we, as an organization that defends marginalized positions in the Israeli-Palestinian conflict, have no media for our defense, cannot reach a larger audience, and can therefore be much more easily silenced, than a more courageous action on your part. It is regrettable that you demonstrated little courage and gave in to force.

We know that some day, when Israeli Apartheid has ended, and the crimes of the state of Israel are internationally condemned, even institutions like the AAI will call Desmond Tutu a model. Until then there is still a long way to go.

Best regards
The Executive Team of Dar al Janub

NOTES TO THE DOCUMENTATION:

All letters translated from German to English by Dar al Janub

Original correspondence:

- *"Die Gemeinde Insider" December 2014 page 19*
- *www.dar-al-janub.net*

Tiberias and the Lake of Gennesaret – 1936

Thanks to the following individuals and institutions:

Opec Fund for International Development (OFID) for funding our project,
Social Charitable Center Society (SCCS) for being our project partners,
and all members, activists, volunteers in SCCS,
Scheikh Hani, Scheikh Adel, Fawwaz Hamad, Helga Baumgarten, Pater Karl Helmreich,
Viktoria Waltz, Maya Jaber, Amina Arfa, Maria-Beate Eder, Joan and Peter Unterweger,
NGO Zochrot, Pax Christi, BDS Austria,
Frauen in Schwarz Wien, Koordinationsforum zur Unterstützung
Palästinas, Palästinensische Jugend Österreich,
Dancing Group Djudhur Filastin.